TRAINING

AND

RACING

BIATHLONS

by Mark Sisson

Primal Urge Press / Los Angeles

TRAINING AND RACING BIATHLONS

A Primal Urge Book / May 1989

Library of Congress Catalog Card Number: 89-091692
ISBN 0-9623067-0-3

Printed in the United States of America

Primal Urge Press
11693 San Vicente Blvd. Suite 172
Los Angeles, CA 90049

ACKNOWLEDGEMENTS

I wish to thank several people for their assistance in this project: Gary Hooker, who has helped translate what comes out of the labs into more practical applications; Rich Graham, who pointed me in the right direction with his editing; Patrick Aroff for his cover design, and Harald Johnson, who designed the interior layout. I am grateful also to the many athletes who have served as my "laboratory animals" over the years. Their dedication and enthusiasm in sticking to the program and showing great results have inspired me to continue to look for ways to make training as effective and fun as possible.

WARNING!

Biathlon training can be beneficial to your health!

Nevertheless, if you are just now beginning an exercise program or are about to take one up where you left off several years ago, it is highly recommended that you have a physical examination by a qualified physician before you begin this or any training program.

CONTENTS

INTRODUCTION

The importance of an effective training program

The sport of biathlon has grown tremendously over the past few years. Its popular run-bike-run format has already attracted hundreds of thousands of participants who see the sport as the ideal test of endurance and human performance. There are currently several hundred biathlons to choose from in the USA, ranging in length from very short "mini" biathlons, to the standard 5k run- 30k bike-5k run, to the "ultras" like the 10k-62k-10k Desert Princess Series in Palm Springs, California. Some marketing studies indicate that biathlon may even overtake triathlon as the most popular multi-event sport of the '80s and '90s.

Biathletes come from every conceivable kind of background. Many new biathletes have crossed over from single sports like running or cycling. Still others have de-evolved from the triathlon, having decided perhaps that swimming was better left to those born with fins and gills. And we are even starting to see high-school athletes whose first experience in competition comes through biathlon. Whatever your origins are and your reasons for competing, this new breed of sport appears to be around for a long while to come.

Presumably, you have decided to become a biathlete because you enjoy riding your bike and you like to run. Those are pretty important prerequisites for this sport! But you are also probably very motivated, goal oriented, interested in aerobic fitness and health in general, and fairly competitive with yourself and with others. And I'll bet that you hate to waste time. In fact, it was my own preoccupation with avoiding wasted time and energy that prompted me to put this program together. After all, if you are going to go out there and try to push the envelope of your own endurance, you want your training to be effective. You certainly don't want to spend time doing something that may actually hinder your progress.

Over the years I have known hundreds of self-coached athletes. Many have been extremely successful at national or world-class levels. Many more, however, have failed to ever achieve their true potential. Frustrated by injuries and overtraining, they eventually leave the sport, discouraged by lack of progress. The difference between success and failure for these athletes was largely a matter of objectivity. The key to coaching yourself is in maintaining an informed objectivity about who you are and what your strengths and weaknesses are. When you know these strengths, when you know how to monitor progress and how to avoid overtraining, you are the most qualified person to coach yourself. When you don't know what to look for, when you don't pay attention to the signs of overtraining, when you do the wrong type of training at the wrong times, you can be your own worst enemy. This program is intended to teach you what types of training to do, when they should be done, how to monitor your progress and when to back off, so that you can become that successful self-coached biathlete.

1

BORN TO RUN AND RIDE

Differences and Similarities

"I yam what I yam and that's alls what I yam."
— Popeye The Sailorman

The human body is the product of evolution. It is a survival machine resulting from millions of positively selected random mutations taking place over millions of years. Our ability to run long distances, to sprint, to store and burn fats, and to become stronger through training are all a result of our remote ancestors having been fit enough to survive the rigors of a hostile environment and pass their genes along to us. Many of those adaptations made through the eons are of little or no practical use to us today. If we run out of food, we drive on down to the 7-11; we aren't automatically forced to survive on stored fat as we migrate to the next nearest food supply. Death and destruction don't, for all intents and purposes, lurk around every corner, requiring that we be prepared to run for our lives several times a day as our ancestors did. Our survival is pretty well assured. As a result, many of us have gone soft.

Fortunately, all of us share the same mechanisms by which adaptations take place over time to make us faster, stronger and more efficient. We all have the same number of muscles and bones connected in the same fashion, we all burn fats the same way, we all produce lactic acid, we all have a brain that recognizes the sensations of pain and exhaustion, and so on. All that information is contained in the DNA of each of us. The difference between individuals is only the degree to which we perform these functions and the absolute limitations to which we can eventually carry them out. Look at any great triathlete or biathlete and you will see an ideal blend of genetics and training. It is not enough to simply be born genetically endowed with a higher degree of those endurance functions. A tremendous amount of well- directed, specific training must be done to bring out an individual's genetic potential. Frequently, this great potential goes unrealized or unfulfilled because of inappropriate training; either too much or too little.

Which brings me to another point. The human body has a marvelous tendency to conserve energy. It is as if that's the primary job of the body. Face it, we are inclined to be couch potatoes. We all tend to store excess calories as fat rather than burn those calories off immediately. The blueprints for manufacturing the enzymes to burn fats are always there in our DNA files, but unless we create some special requirement for that extra energy, the enzymes that burn fat are never synthesized or, at best, are made only in minute quantities, and the body continues to store rather than spend. Likewise, if we don't use our muscles regularly, they'll atrophy, because even resting muscles burn fuel and it would be inefficient to have any unnecessary muscle tissue burning precious fuel. As athletes, we must constantly be creating the need for our bodies to change. We must invent specific reasons for our body-machines to take that genetic information and put it to use, implement it, adapt it to our unique biathlon "survival" situation.

THE PERFECT RACE

Surely everyone who competes has dreamed of the

perfect race - the day when it all comes together, the world record, the gold medal, or simply winning your age group or defeating your training partner. The final outcome of your perfect race may differ from everyone else, but the physiological processes will be remarkably similar. The perfect race is a result of all the systems in our body working at their peak:

● neuromuscular patterning for optimum technique so there is no wasted energy

● complete muscle fiber recruitment so that all muscles involved are sharing the load

● a strong oxygen delivery system, assuring that fats and carbohydrates are being burned aerobically

● the necessary fat mobilizing and metabolizing enzymes

● capillary proliferation supplying every muscle fiber with fuel and carrying away waste products

● glycogen being burned aerobically as tinder for fat metabolism, and anaerobically at a rate that will allow for the greatest speed, paced so that it will be exhausted just prior to the finish of the race but not so great that too much lactic acid accumulates and slows us down just before the finish

● an electrolyte balance that, thanks to our ongoing-consumption of fluid, stays even and prevents cramping and overheating

● efficient hormone production and feedback to control all these functions

● the mental ability to stay focused enough to distinguish between pain and exhaustion.

These and countless other "systems" are working over-time during a race to propel you faster towards that finish line. Sound complicated? It is, and yet we can train specifically for each and every one of these systems.

THE SYSTEMS APPROACH

The athlete can only be as strong as his weakest link. The consummate biathlete can not afford to rely totally on only one aspect of performance. Great endurance with no speed won't produce optimum results, nor will relying solely on fabulous cycling technique or superior ability to push through mental barriers. Instead, the biathlete must train each and every one of those systems which contribute to his ability to sustain a high work output and race faster. As a result, he must take a systems approach to his training, sometimes isolating a particular "ingredient" and some-times combining several, but continually focusing on all the contributing elements, not just the obvious few.

It's important to begin to understand some key con-cepts about how the body works and why certain re-sponses occur. This way, we can begin to understand why certain types of training can be done effectively only when other goals or physiological milestones have been met, why there is a logical order to endurance training, and why, in some cases, doing certain workouts before you are ready can actually impede your progress towards a race season peak!

2

BASIC BIATHLON
TRAINING THEORY

What You Don't Know CAN Hurt You

In all living organisms, a stimulus/response reaction occurs at the cellular level, whereby a stress applied to a cell, an enzyme system, or a muscle (and, hence, an entire organism) will generally cause the organism to respond by becoming stronger. This is known as the GENERAL ADAPTATION PRINCIPAL. If the stress is too great, the cell dies; if not enough, no adaptation occurs because none is necessary. Similarly, if the rest (recovery) period is too short before another stress is applied (as when an athlete is overtrained), the cell will break down from the accumulated effects of the stress. If the rest period is too long, any adaptation is lost through ATROPHY. It is often a very fine line between positive adaptation and breakdown, and on a grand scale this distinction differs with each individual.

The fine line between adaptation and breakdown is precisely where we want our training to occur. We want to create just enough stress to cause a positive adaptation, yet not so much that breakdown occurs through overtraining. There are three general criteria we can use to determine what is enough and what is too much. It is the unique mix of workload (INTENSITY), how long your workouts or interval sessions last (DURATION), and how often you do them (FREQUENCY), that provides the basis for an effective training strategy.

The choice of workloads in training should also be specific to the type of work done in racing. SPECIFICITY of training workload is the reason a Tour de France cyclist does not automatically make a great distance runner, even though he is certainly an aerobic athlete and trains nearly the same muscles. It's simple. To run well you have to spend time running. To be a good hill climber, you must specifically train on hills. To run well in the heat, you should plan your workouts for the warmest part of the day. A training plan that pays close attention to specificity will eventually focus on every possible aspect of racing. For that reason, we can even distinguish between short course and long course biathlon training schedules.

Another way to ride that fine training line without going over the edge is to pay attention to PERIODICITY. Our long-term plan of training and racing will force the body to work overtime to repair and build. No one can sustain a peak race condition for very long without incorporating at least a little rest. Periodicity suggests that we alternate some periods of intense work with some periods of lighter work or rest. This applies from week to week, race to race and season to season.

When all of the systems we discussed earlier are working at their peak during a race, the biathlete's single most important concern is his ability to take in oxygen and transport it to the muscle cells. This is known as AEROBIC CAPACITY. Most of our training involves some means of trying to increase that ability. The absolute greatest amount of oxygen that your body can process at a given time is called MAXIMAL AEROBIC CAPACITY or VO2 MAX. This figure is determined in the laboratory by measuring inhaled and exhaled oxygen and carbon dioxide. It is usually expressed relative to your body weight in milliliters per kilogram per minute. The range of VO2 MAX for trained athletes can be anywhere from 45 ml/kg to 85 ml/kg and even higher in some world class biathletes. Our goal in training is to raise VO2 MAX to as high as we possibly can by eventually training at intensities close to that VO2 MAX. For each of us, there is a genetic limit to how high we can raise our VO2 MAX. With effective

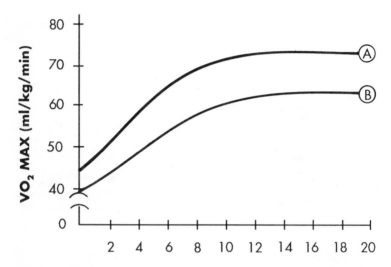

FIGURE 1. Changes in VO2 MAX for two biathletes training 20 weeks at intensities ranging from 75 percent to 100 percent of VO2 MAX HR.
Note that after a few months of this level of training, both Biathlete **A** and Biathlete **B** improve considerably but reach a point where no further increase occurs. This is due to the fact that each of us probably has a built-in genetic limit to how high we can raise VO2 MAX.

training we can usually reach that peak within a few months (Figure 1).

At low levels of work, most of our energy comes from the aerobic burning of FATS. One of the most important "skills" we develop as endurance athletes is the ability to burn fats at a relatively high rate for long periods of time during races, thereby sparing another precious fuel called GLYCOGEN. This ability is critical because, if glycogen stores become depleted, the muscles basically stop working. The more fats we can burn at an aerobic pace, the more glycogen we can save for later and avoid the dreaded "WALL." Figure 2 shows the relative contribution of fats and carbohydrates (of which glycogen is one form) during a race at an aerobic pace.

Unfortunately, as the intensity of pace increases, the body eventually cannot continue to supply enough oxygen for aerobic work and ANAEROBIC mechanisms are called

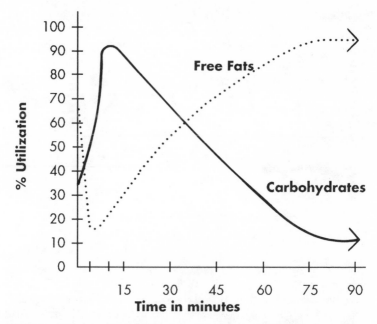

FIGURE 2. *Relative contribution of fats and carbohydrates as fuel during a race.*
At rest, fats are utilized to a higher degree than carbohydrates (glycogen). As the gun goes off, the early minutes of a race involve a much higher contribution of carbohydrate fuel as the muscles warm up, until aerobic mechanisms "kick in." As the race progresses, the relative contribution of fat as fuel increases dramatically. At the same time, as glycogen stores are slowly depleted, the relative contribution of carbohydrate dimishes. The biathlete who can burn fats more efficiently will have an advantage, since once glycogen stores are depleted, the ball game is over.

— *Adapted from "A Scientific Approach to Distance Running" by David Costill*

in to assist. Anaerobic energy production takes place in the absence of oxygen and can only be effective for very short periods of time (like less than a minute if you are going all-out). One of the by-products of anaerobic energy production is LACTIC ACID, which accumulates in the bloodstream and interferes with the efficiency of any ongoing aerobic processes. Since our races all last considerably longer than a few minutes, we are wise to avoid any build-up of this lactic acid (also known as LACTATE) in the early stages of our racing or our longer training sessions. Our goal is to stay at the high end of our aerobic capacity. Although some anaerobic processes are always going on at low levels, there is a point at which these processes increase drastically. We call the point where your body produces more lactic acid than it can comfortably accommodate or recycle back into the system, the ANAEROBIC THRESH-OLD or (AT). This threshold point can be measured in the laboratory by analysis of blood lactates or it can be esti-mated in the field in a rather simple controlled test (p. 28). Another primary goal of the biathlete is to raise the AT through training and then to race at or just below that threshold (Figure 3). The good news is that even if your genetic VO2 MAX is relatively low, you can raise your AT through proper training and keep up with or even beat athletes who have a higher VO2 MAX but a low threshold.

One final word on anaerobic threshold. It is actually only represented by a point on a curve. Training can push that curve out there and cause that point to be associated with a higher workload and a higher heart rate. But it is still on a curve. In longer races, you will probably not be able to maintain a pace that is at your AT. At best, it will be near your AT but somewhere lower on the curve. The final test of your racing fitness and what determines how close to your AT you can race will be your LACTATE TOLER-ANCE. This is simply your ability to withstand increas-ingly greater amounts of lactic acid and not have it slow you down (Figure 4). The latter stages of training will involve occasional repeated bouts of aerobic/anaerobic work, called INTERVALS. Here you will be producing relatively large amounts of lactic acid in short bursts and then allowing your body to recover briefly in order to recycle the lactic acid. The end result will be an increase in lactate tolerance and your ability to race at the higher end of your anaerobic threshold.

Throughout this book, I will refer to workloads and

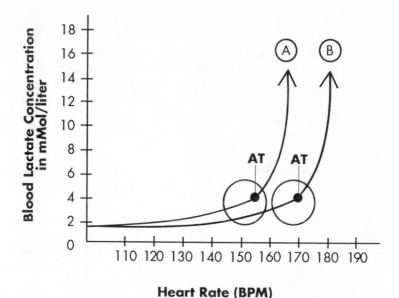

FIGURE 3. *Training at heart rates of 85 percent to 95 percent VO₂ MAX HR can raise your anaerobic threshold.*

A represents the amounts of lactates produced by Joe Biathlete before training. Note that at a heart rate of 155 he has reached 4 mMol/liter which is recognized as the standard for anaerobic threshold. The circle encloses what, more realistically, could be called the threshold zone. If he were to race long races, he would probably race at a heart rate slightly lower on the curve. For shorter races, he could sustain a slightly higher HR and therefore higher lactic acid concentrations. B represents the same athlete after 20 weeks of training. He has pushed the entire curve to the right. Now he doesn't hit his threshold until 170 beats a minute and his threshold zone is also higher. This means he can sustain a faster race pace without going anaerobic.

training intensities as a function of heart rate. As work-loads increase, your heart rate increases nearly linearly up to your VO2 MAX. It is much more reliable to assign workloads in terms of a percentage of maximum heart rate than it is to arbitrarily assign mile times or miles-per-hour pace on the bike. We will define maximum heart rate (100% HR) as the heart rate you generate at VO2 MAX and we will actually determine that number shortly. Under this definition, aerobic work will range from 65 percent up to 100 percent and anaerobic work will sometimes call for

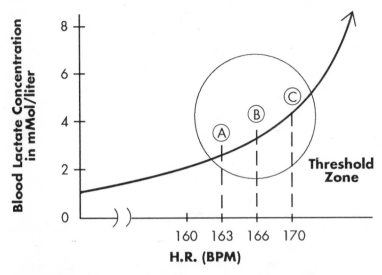

FIGURE 4. The effects of aerobic/anaerobic speedwork on lactate tolerance.
As noted previously in FIG. 3, Joe Biathlete has raised his anaerobic threshold heart rate **C** to 170 beats per minute. However, his lactate tolerance is not great. In a $2^1/_2$-hour race, he is only able to sustain an average heart rate **A** of 163 beats per minute. After 6 weeks of speedwork, he has increased his lactate tolerance to the point **B** where he can now sustain 166 beats per minute and, therefore, a faster pace.

heart rates of 105 percent or 110 percent. The absolute best way to accurately monitor your heart rate during workouts is to use a device called, strangely enough, a heart rate monitor. There are several on the market now ranging in price from $140.00 to over $300.00. I highly recommend obtaining one. It can take a great deal of the guesswork out of your training.

Another reason for monitoring your heart is to help determine your recovery cycles. A high RESTING PULSE or resting heart rate, may be a sign of overtraining, or, at very least, a sign that you are not yet recovered from a previous hard workout. Recovery time from workouts is not a common denominator among athletes. What works for some people will not work for others. Some athletes may only need 18 to 24 hours to recover from hard workouts. Most of us require on the order of 48 to 72. This is not a sign of weakness but a genetic fact of life. The point is stick to your own schedule, not someone else's. When your friends' workouts coincide, do them together. Otherwise, let them follow your routine, don't follow theirs.

Generally, you will find that as your fitness improves so does your health (defined as absence of illness). However, don't automatically assume that the more fit you become, the healthier you will remain. Achieving peak fitness requires some significant training stresses. When your body breaks down from training, as it must in order to stimulate a positive adaptation, muscle tissue competes with your immune system for nutrients and rest. Poor nutrition or inadequate recovery from workouts will cause both your immune system and your fitness to decline. This often results in illness or injury, which will in turn cause a further decline in fitness (Figure 5). However, if you pay attention to the warning signs, monitor HR and know your recovery cycles, you can easily avoid this common trap.

Another way to avoid that trap is to approach your training as a collection of individual workouts and not as an accumulation of weekly mileage. There are three basic categories of workouts in this program. Each category addresses a specific training goal. BREAKTHROUGH (BT) workouts are the meat of the program. These are the true work sessions that provide most of your training stress. Each BT should be done with the intent of achieving some new incremental level of fitness for the rest of the season. Over time, improvement in BTs can come in the form of more distance or of greater intensity. Every BT should be rested for and planned in advance. Two or three good BTs a week are all you need to improve fitness. The rest is just filler. BREAK-EVEN (BE) workouts are lower intensity, lower mileage workouts that contribute to your fitness by maintaining what you have gained in breakthroughs. Whereas BTs generally have an immediate or short term (ACUTE) response, BEs contribution is more of a long term (CUMULATIVE) effect. The goal of a BE day is to either take it easy after a BT day, or to rest up (while still training) for an upcoming BT. The third category of

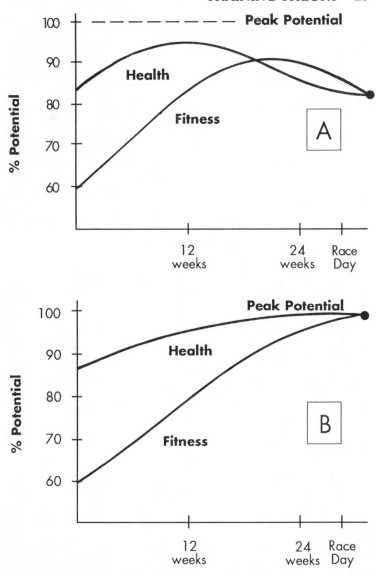

FIGURE 5. Health and fitness are interrelated.

In graph **A**, a classic case of overtraining has caused this athlete's health to decline, even though fitness kept improving for a while. After several weeks, illness and injury catch up causing a decline in fitness that will take several weeks to regain. This could be avoided. In **B**, the athlete has paid attention to recovery cycles, periodicity and has closely monitored his progress daily. He shows up at the starting line race day in peak fitness and peak health.

workout is ACTIVE RECOVERY (AR). AR workouts are very low level, low mileage, therapeutic recovery workouts. It has been shown that very low levels of aerobic activity can contribute more to recovery than some periods of time taken off completely. AR workouts do have a specific purpose, but stress is definitely not it. Always categorize your intended workouts as either BT, BE or AR. Avoid the temptation to do workouts that have no obvious purpose other than to look good on your weekly mileage chart. If a workout has no specific purpose, it's junk mileage.

3

EVALUATING YOUR FITNESS

A Starting Point

Everyone starts from some level of fitness, whether it is at zero or near peak. In order to begin to put a plan of action together for racing and training, it is important to evaluate you present level of fitness and begin to recognize what type of specific work is needed to bring you to your race goals, as well as what workloads you can safely handle without breaking down. Some initial evaluations are easy. If you are coming off a previous season of racing, you are probably quite ready to roll. Perhaps you have a strong background in cycling but no running experience. In that case, an immediate general evaluation would indicate that the first few months of your program should focus much more heavily on running. More specific evaluations occur as your training begins and you notice strengths and weaknesses.

Keeping a log is the most effective way of recording your progress so that you can continually re-evaluate and notice what works and what doesn't, over time. This record- keeping need not be a burdensome, time-consuming task. Some simple parameters recorded daily are all you really need. But monitoring these parameters IS one of the most important parts of this program, so please do it! A sample page appears at the end of this book. Photocopy it as a format for your logbook or invent your own version.

At first, you will want to record simple parameters like your weight, resting pulse, and VO2 MAX HR. Then put down recent race PRs as well as any PRs over your cycling and running training courses. If you have had any lab tests like a MAX VO2, bodyfat, or cholesterol done recently, record those. As you progress, record changes in all these parameters. Monitoring will allow you to adjust your baseline so that workloads can continue to increase progressively.

INITIAL EVALUATIONS

Estimating VO2 MAX Heart Rate

The old rule of 220 minus your age just isn't very accurate when you get right down to it. My friend Gary Hooker, a top biathlete at 47, has devised a very easy and surprisingly accurate means of determining VO2 MAX HR, employing the research of David Costill and Gerry Purdy and James Gardner. As Gary says, if you don't know your maximal heart rate, it does you no good to use a heart monitor for training.

Basically, the heart rate you generate at the end of an evenly paced, all-out, five to eight minute time trial to exhaustion is MAX HR. Refer to the Fractional Pace Chart in Appendix 1 and go down the first column under 10k until you find a time that is nearest your most recent all-out 10k. If you don't have a 10k time, look under 5k or 10 mile. Otherwise, for now, just guess what kind of 10k shape you're in. Once you find that time, go across that same line horizontally until you are under the VO2 MAX test-pace column heading. The number on that line is the per-mile pace you should do your test at. (Next to it is that same pace, broken down into 1/4 mile track pace).

Lace up those shoes and go out to the track. Make sure you are well rested the day you do your test. Warm up with an easy mile or two. Using a heart monitor to show your ongoing heart rate and a stopwatch (chronograph), begin running at the pace indicated on the chart. It is very important to run at an even pace, so having someone at the track to call splits would be advised, or better yet, use one of those pace watches that beeps every ten seconds or so. If you have selected the proper test pace, you should be able to complete at least four laps and probably no more than eight laps before exhaustion forces you to slow down. Remember, when you slow down, the test is over. If you can't finish four, stop the test and try again another day at a slower pace. The key during the test is to hold pace. No finish sprinting is allowed. Now this is important: Look at your monitor as you are nearing exhaustion. The HR you are showing just prior to exhaustion is your VO2 MAX HR and is the number you will be working with in terms of training loads and percentages all season. When I say run at 85 percent HR, you will be looking for a heart rate that is 85 percent of the MAX HR you just determined. If your MAX HR is 185, then 85 percent would be 157 beats per minute. Your MAX HR number will not change this season with training, it is a factor of age and genetics. However, your maximum oxygen uptake (your VO2 MAX) WILL CHANGE, and that is what we want!

This same test can be conducted on a stationary bicycle under similar conditions; all-out, evenly paced for five to eight minutes. The key would also be to pick a pace that you can sustain for at least five but no more than eight minutes. An outdoors test is impractical due to the logistics of finding an exactly marked-off, flat bike course. Generally, your running VO2 MAX yields the most accurate results. I've even tried this on a treadmill, where you can really establish an even pace, and it works quite well. Just do it in a cool or ventilated room, because heat artificially drives up the HR. And for some reason, the pace you select on a treadmill should be 15 - 30 seconds per mile slower to take you to exhaustion. Good luck and PLEASE do this test.

Estimating Max According To Perceived Effort

If you don't own a heart monitor, it begins to get a little difficult to be certain you are within optimum training HR ranges referred to in these workouts. It is possible to stop and take a quick 10-second pulse count at the end of your MAX test and multiply by six. However, that can be off by 12 or more beats either way, and trying to take a pulse count for verification during a hard bike workout can be impractical or dangerous. If you are dead set against caving into high-tech, there is another possibility for gauging your workload. It is very subjective and less precise, but it can be used as a measuring tool. George Sheehan has called it the PERCEIVED EFFORT SCALE. With apologies to George, my own interpretation of it, for purposes of our discussion here, is an ascending scale from 1 - 10 of your perception of the difficulty of effort while riding or running. 1 would be the effort involved in standing still, 2 the effort of a slow walk, 5 your easiest jog or a Sunday ride in the park. 10 would be that all out (100 percent) effort of a VO2 MAX HR test. Therefore, a 9 on your perceived effort scale would equal 90 percent, 8 = 80 percent, 7 = 70 percent, etc. So, for example, if I suggest a long steady ride at 70 percent HR, you would, after some warm-up period, keep your perceived effort level at 7. As your fitness improves, your perception of effort should also change in accordance with it, so there will be no reason to re-adjust your scale.

Whatever your means of evaluating MAX HR, know that number or that sensation "by heart" and use it as a benchmark for all your training efforts.

ONGOING EVALUATIONS - REASSESSING FITNESS

Submaximal Test - Is your training working?

A submaximal test can be useful over the long haul in determining if your training is being effective, and in the short term to detect possible overtraining. Many athletes use a "submax" test prior to a hard interval workout to determine whether or not they should even be doing that workout that day. It is a simple, quick, painless test that some people even use as part of a warm up. Like some of the other tests, though, it does require a stopwatch and a heart monitor. You can't really do the test without these.

Refer again to the Fractional Pace Chart in Appendix 1 Again locate your 10k PR or current 5k or 10 mile time. Follow that line all the way across to the last column, the sub-max column. That will show your pace per mile at roughly 75 - 85 percent of your MAX HR. It is an estimate and that particular pace probably covers a wide range of PR performance levels. Whatever the submax test pace you select, use that same pace throughout the season and from year to year for ongoing comparison, even though you become so fit that this pace seems laughable. It is your benchmark.

The test is basically the same as the VO2 MAX HR test. Just run an evenly paced mile on the track at your submax pace and record your heart rate during the final 100 meters. That's it. You're done. Take that number and divide it by your MAX HR. This percentage represents your "submaximal efficiency." Keep track of this from week to week. If your training is working for you, this figure should drop over time. If it happens to rise appreciably from one week to another, you are probably overtraining. It is a very reliable indicator of improvement in performance. Do this test often if you can. Twice a week just before BT workouts is optimal.

As an example, let's say that Joe Biathlete has a MAX HR of 180. Since his 10k PR is 37:30, he sees on the chart that his submax test pace is 7:00. As he begins a season of training, he does a submax test and finishes with a HR of 144. He figures his submax efficiency at 80 percent (144 divided by 180 equals 80 percent), and records it in his journal. He does the test every week before a long run or before a hard BT interval session. Two months into his training program, Joe can do his submax test at 126 HR, so his maximal efficiency number is dropping (126 divided by 180 equals 70 percent, which means that he is only using 70 percent of his capacity to run that test mile now, versus 80 percent a few months ago), and he knows his aerobic efficiency is improving. However, after two very hard weeks of training during the speed phase, he notices that his test HR is 138 one day. He reviews his training log and realizes he has been overtraining. As a result, he skips the scheduled workout for that day, and takes the next day off as well. Carefully, he puts in a couple of BE days and then does the submax test again. Back to his 126 HR once again, he resumes his regular schedule. This time he will avoid overtraining by cutting down the duration and intensity of his BT workouts.

CONCONI TEST:

Estimating Anaerobic Threshold (AT)

For those of you who are true "monitoring" fanatics, there is a test you can do outside the laboratory to actually measure anaerobic threshold. Not everyone can get usable results from this test, but those who do find it provides just one more bit of valuable feedback information as to how their training is progressing.

Developed several years ago, this test was based on Francesco Conconi's observation that, as workload and heart rate increase, lactic acid builds up exponentially. The point at which lactic rises appreciably is also associated with a deflection in the curve representing the heart rate response to the increased load. In other words, according to Conconi, your heart rate will increase somewhat linearly with increased loads at low intensities, but at some point begins to flatten out as lactates build up. If you plot workload versus heart rate on a graph, the point where that straight line starts to fatten out correlates to your anaerobic threshold heart rate. Knowing your AT will put you that much closer to defining the narrow range of optimal training as you get to the strength and speed phases of this program. Doing a Conoconi test every month or so is a way to determine whether you are actually improving AT. (Of course race results are also pretty good indicators). The test is a little complicated, but provides one more tool for refining your training.

As mentioned previously, to raise AT it is necessary to spend some periods of time training at or near 100 percent of your anaerobic threshold. This usually correlates to between 85 and 95 percent of your MAX HR. However, if you know your AT, you can narrow your training range down even more accurately to that range which is just 10 percent below your current AT heart rate. For example, if the Conconi test suggests AT HR is 160 beats per minute, then your optimum training range for raising AT further would be 144 - 160 (10 percent of 160 = 16, 160 -16 = 144.)

The Conconi test is not done to exhaustion like the Max test. It is another submaximal test. Get a trackstand or wind trainer and set your bike up with a straight-block freewheel (12-13-14-15-16-17-18). You'll also need a heart monitor and a cyclometer attached to your rear wheel. Pump your rear tire and record the pressure for future reference (you'll want the same tire pressure each time you do the test). Now make sure that your tire's rolling resistance is constant by pedaling your bike on the trainer steadily at 15 mph and then letting the rear wheel come to a complete stop while you time it. Adjust the resistance of your wheel against the wind trainer roller assembly until you get a consistent 4 seconds (plus or minus .5) coasting to a stop. Now you are ready.

Warm up for 15 to 20 minutes in an easy gear, gradually shifting up through the higher gears and back again to lower gears so you are only spinning easily at the end of the warm up. Have an assistant there to write down numbers as you call them out and to tell you when to proceed to the next step. In a medium-range gear, begin pedaling and stabilize the speed on the cyclocomputer readout to 10 mph. Have your assistant start the stopwatch, and as soon as it hits 45-50 seconds, read and call out the heart rate so he can record it. He should immediately (at 50 seconds) tell you to increase speed to 11 mph. Take 5 or 10 seconds to do that and hold 11 mph for another 45-50 seconds, at the end of which you will give your new heart rate, he will record it and tell you to move up to 12 mph. Continue increasing your speed in 1 mph increments, holding 45 - 50 seconds and allowing 10 seconds to accelerate so that you are reading HR at 60 second intervals. Do this until you can feel appreciable amounts of lactic acid building up in your legs and stop the test.

On a sheet of graph paper, plot your results. Make the vertical axis your heart rate and the horizontal axis your speed (see the example in Appendix 2). You can make your curve more apparent by squaring the speed on that horizontal axis (10 mph squared = 100, 11 squared equals 121, 12 = 144. etc.). Now plot your heart rate versus your speed and notice that the points form basically a straight line at lower speeds. As your speed increases, however, the line should begin to bend noticeably. Draw two straight lines through the points on your graph; one line through the earliest set of points and one through the points defining the latter stages of your test. That point where the two lines intersect, where the bend occurs, corresponds to your heart rate at AT. Follow that point straight across your graph to find that heart rate. Record that heart rate in your log and use it for the next month as your AT reference point. When you test again, your AT should have risen somewhat. Now use that new number as your reference point.

As I mentioned before, this is useful information to have, but it is not absolutely necessary to your obtaining optimal results. If you find this test confusing or you cannot get usable results, skip it and stick to the submax test.

4

GOAL SETTING

Making Your List and Checking it Twice

RACE GOALS

What do you feel you are capable of? Be realistic about your goals. A lot of us might entertain the fantasy of winning the Ironman. But the harsh reality is that years of preparation and a tremendous amount of training are necessary to even consider such a goal. It may not be realistic from the standpoint of your ultimate genetic potential, your present age or your level of commitment. On the other hand, there are many significant, attainable goals that can be within your immediate grasp.

I think it's wise to have in mind a long-term goal, sort of halfway between fantasy and reality. One that you know in your heart you could achieve if everything went perfectly in training and you had that once-in-a-lifetime day. In order to move towards that goal, build a series of more immediate short-term goals, milestones if you will, from race to race or even workout to workout. These are usually as simple as lowering your overall times, or taking so many minutes off that final run leg or bike course on a standardized biathlon route. As your season unfolds, each new goal can build upon the successful completion of a previous one.

Now find a schedule of races for the coming year and

pick all the races you think you would like to compete in. In some cases you may find conflicts in your work or family schedule, or maybe you find two or more races scheduled the same weekend. Refine the list to those races you realistically know you can attend. Now prioritize the races on your list. Call your highest priority races, the ones you feel you absolutely must do well in, your "A" list. Ideally you should have no more than four races on your "A" list, since these races require the most focus and specific work, and will take the most out of you if you race them in peak condition. They should also fall more towards the end of the season to take advantage of your progressive increase in fitness. So start to plan your season accordingly.

Your medium priority, or "B" list, can be a little longer. These races should be spaced well enough apart not to conflict with any "A" races. "B" races are the indicators of how your training is working for you from week to week or month to month. Finally, you might be willing to do a few races just for the experience or as training days. This is the "C" list and should generally consist of any early season races you have chosen.   "C" races can even be optional so that you can choose to do them, or cancel them, depending on how your training is progressing. One key rule is that ALL races should be done because you WANT to do them and not because you feel you HAVE to do them because of some pre-set schedule.

GENERAL TRAINING GOALS

Now that we have a starting point assessment of fitness and a proposed list of races, we can begin to focus on the specific nature of training necessary to improve fitness and accomplish the race goals. There is a general action-plan, a progression of physiological milestones that you should follow to maximize your training. But there are also some specific training details unique to you that require your monitoring progress and noting where you need work within the framework of the general plan. In other words, some of us may be able to bring our aerobic capacity up to speed in a very short while but need extra work on leg strength. Others have much of the required strength but take more time to build an aerobic base. These sorts of differences will appear obvious to you as you begin to work into the program. There are also some important general training goals which I will cover now.

One of the key factors in a successful training program is the ability to keep the workouts interesting and fun. This doesn't mean they can't be challenging. On the contrary, challenge is another very important component. But there must be an element of creativity, newness and discovery in the work you do. Familiarity can be comforting, but riding the same old bike course or running the same loop day in and day out loses appeal quickly. With it go motivation and dedication. The workouts I list are only suggestions; you will soon get the idea about the intention of a particular session and should substitute what works for you. So whatever your specific workload mission is on a particular training day, always look to see how you can spice it up, make it visually exciting with new terrain, or invent a new interval distance.

Another general training goal is to be sure that the work you are doing is progressive, and that over time you are able to perform better, faster and more efficiently. This may sound all too obvious, but think for a minute how often you see friends doing the same workouts at the exact same pace week in and week out during the season. This is probably not progressive. Maybe Tuesday is always track day for these friends, always quarters and always at 75 - 78 seconds apiece. This is a common training rut, primarily due to a lack of specific direction, and it is easy to fall into. When you train with a group of individuals with various degrees of expertise, you only wind up doing an average of everyone's optimum workout. So every once in a while, do a "progression analysis" with your training and be sure that you are truly performing better over the long haul when you do repeats of workouts. And do your submaximal test frequently.

Another way to avoid that trap is to ask yourself, "What is my purpose in doing this particular workout?" Find one or two very specific goals of each workout and work with those in mind. In fact, record those goals in your log before you actually do them and then compare your results when finished. This doesn't mean that every workout needs to be a hard, fast, quality (BT) session. Sometimes it is just as important to set a goal to go slow, easy and short as when "active recovery" (AR) is called for or when working on technique. We'll get into what other specific goals you might have shortly.

One of the most important aspects of the program to remember is that the focus must be on individual workouts - not on miles per week. If you can grasp this concept, you will immediately be miles ahead of the competition. After your base has been established, most of your gains will come from the stimulus provided by each of several key workouts. There will be an acute (immediate) response to the individual stress as well as a cumulative (long term) response to the collection of stresses. You will find it is impossible to train hard every day and derive a positive adaptation. Training hard every day simply does not allow enough rest. (Remember the General Adaptation Principal.) Therefore, another training goal is to schedule your training week so you have a couple of BREAKTHROUGH WORKOUTs (BT) and a couple of BREAK-EVEN WORKOUTS (BE) and no wasted "junk" workouts. Junk workouts are those workouts you do for no other reason than to accumulate mileage. Junk workouts lead directly to overtraining. A breakthrough workout, on the other hand, is one which you have planned and rested for, which if properly done will leave you a notch up in fitness for the rest of the season. A break-even workout is one which simply allows you to maintain fitness without tearing you down and without interfering with a breakthrough day.

On break-even or rest days you should focus on recovery, staying rested and preparing yourself to work hard on those few important breakthrough days. Breakthrough workouts are mini milestones and should be done with intense focus and the knowledge that your reward is an easy day or two afterwards.

SPECIFIC TRAINING GOALS

Although many peripheral systems previously mentioned will contribute to your ability to race well, we will focus on a simple plan of action that addresses the most important of those (see figure 6):

1) ESTABLISHING AEROBIC BASE

2) RAISING VO2 MAX

3) RAISING ANAEROBIC THRESHOLD (AT)

4) INCREASING LACTATE TOLERANCE

There is a logical sequence to follow that assures that we maximize our potential in each of these parameters. Just as you don't paint a house before you lay the foundation, you don't put the finishing touches on a training program without first establishing a base. Without providing adequate nutrient supply and waste removal, we will not be able to maximize endurance later in the season. It is only after we establish certain capillary pathways and increase fat metabolism by doing specific forms of low-level aerobic work that we can move on towards maximizing our aerobic capacity. Then, after establishing that base, we can ultimately train our VO2 MAX to reach a certain genetic limit. After that, we can try to raise our anaerobic threshold to as high a percentage of that VO2 MAX as possible, but, theoretically, we can only go to 100 percent

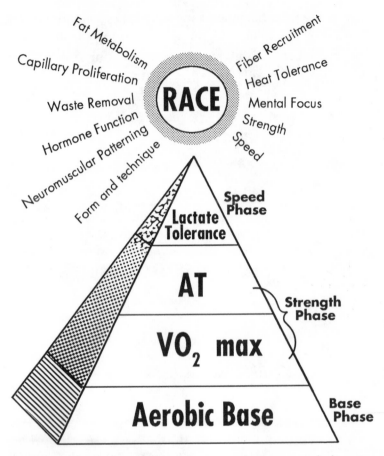

FIGURE 6. A solid training season addresses the many peripheral systems involved in racing by focusing on four major objectives.

(realistically it will be more like 85 to 95 percent.) The final major parameter is our ability to withstand increasingly greater amounts of lactates at or beyond our anaerobic threshold, and it is important to have fully developed both AT and VO2 MAX before exploring that final test.

With this sequence in mind, we can begin to actually plan an entire season of training, racing and rest. Such a plan incorporates all the principals of specificity, periodicity, frequency, intensity and duration. Your own plan of action should reflect the racing schedule you made earlier and allow for plenty of time to train to your peak before doing your "A" list races. The chart on page 38 (figure 7) will give you an idea of what the complete picture looks like and how your fitness potential should increase over time.

Depending on your level of fitness, you should allow 8-12 weeks for the base phase of training, 6-8 weeks for the strength phase, and 4-6 weeks for the speed phase. Plan on maintaining your racing peak for two or three months.

Finally, always allow a couple of months to rest and take it easy. There are too many instances of "burn-out" because an athlete sees the possibility of racing year-round. The body simply can't perform well at high intensities for long periods of time. This doesn't mean you have to become a couch potato, however. Many biathletes use the off-season to explore new sports, ride a mountain bike, ski or hike. The idea is to get the mind off racing and hard training for a while and let the body recover. But enough about vacations. On to the real work!

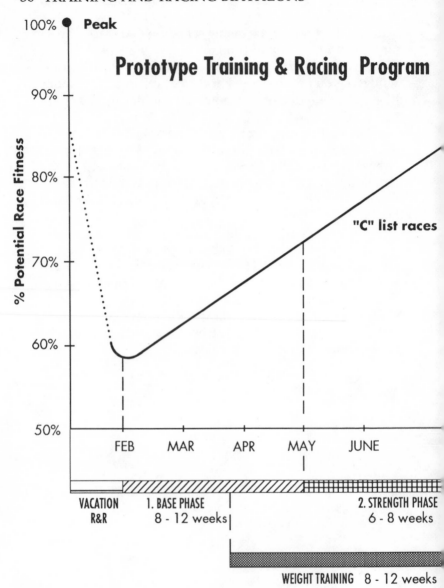

FIGURE 7.

1. BASE PHASE: Develop capillary pathways, fat burning capability, start MAX VO2 work (chapter 5)
2. STRENGTH PHASE: Raise MAX VO2, raise AT (chapter 6)
3. SPEED PHASE: Peak MAX VO2, peak AT, increase lactate tolerance (chapter 7)
4. TAPER: Recover to reach 100% fitness potential (chapter 9)

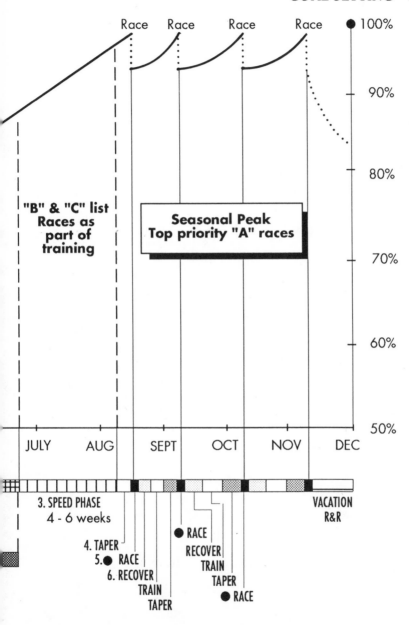

5. RACE: Choose up to 4 or 5 key races to peak for (chapter 10)
Every race will cause a short term decrease in fitness.
6. RECOVER: Specific plan to recover from race before resuming training (chapter 11)

5

THE BASE PHASE

Building a Strong Foundation

Coming off your vacation, the work begins with the re-establishment of the base. Having taken that time easy or off has caused a few changes in the body. By not going out and sustaining long efforts, your body has decided to shut down some of the now-unnecessary capillaries that used to feed muscle cells. In addition, there has been no recent requirement for a huge amount of fat-burning enzymes to complete long rides or runs. Remember that the body's job is to conserve energy, not waste it. So those enzymes, which have a half-life in the body, have diminished in number. Muscle mitochondria, the powerhouse of the cell, have atrophied or diminished. Maybe your weight has even gone up. This is normal. Don't worry about it, because in a month or so, all these energy saving changes will be reversed as we begin to put new demands on all the systems we gave time-off to. This is the base-building period.

Establishing a strong base is extremely important because everything you do the rest of the season depends upon and builds from that base. If you are starting from scratch, the base period not only encourages the laying down of new capillary pathways and creates the need for synthesizing more fat mobilizing and burning enzymes, it also allows you to get used to the daily demands of cycling and running. If your background is running, perhaps you will spend a bit more time during the base phase focusing on your cycling. The opposite will hold true if you are a former bike specialist. Specificity begins immediately. A word of caution to the beginning runner: Running places a higher level of stress on the joints than you may be used to. So be careful to monitor minor aches and pains and treat them as potential injuries until you are more comfortable with daily running. The alternate choice of cycling during these times is one of the many benefits of cross-training.

If this is your first season as a biathlete, allow up to 12 weeks of good, solid base preparation before you "graduate" to the strength phase of training. If, on the other hand, this is your second or third season of biathlon training, you may find that eight weeks is sufficient time to re-establish the base you lost during the off-season. One great saving grace about endurance training is that once you have been fit, it is a lot easier to get that fitness back than it was getting there the first time. Please remember to remain patient during the base phase, though. Don't jump the gun just because you are starting to feel the strength return. This is a long-term program and it's a long season. If you exercise the discipline to do things in the proper sequence, you'll stay fit, healthy and uninjured and you will be able to peak at the appropriate times. And your training will be the most effective. Train too hard, too soon, and you will actually be limiting how far you can progress during the season.

Base training is done at heart rates ranging from 65 - 85 percent MAX HR. Start the first few weeks at the lower end (65 percent), and over the weeks, gradually work toward sustaining HRs at the higher end. The optimum way to control these workouts during both the run and the bike sessions is to wear a heart monitor during the workout and simply determine a range within which you intend to stay. The important number is actually the high end of the range. Once you establish that number (see evaluation Chapter 3), try not to exceed it during the ride or run. If you find yourself trying to keep up with a group or a friend and your HR starts to climb, back off and stay within your goal range. Believe me, I am well aware that this is one of the most difficult things for a naturally "competitive" person to do, but the time will come soon enough when you will get to push the limits. Do YOUR workouts, not someone else's'.

For the base period, the fitness goals are several:

● develop cardiovascular efficiency

● create the neuromuscular patterning that will enable you to push harder later on

● get used to spending longer periods of time running or riding, as well as the ability to recover as quickly as possible and be able to train the next day

● encourage the synthesis of enzymes involved in fat metabolism

● promote the growth and proliferation of capillaries in and around the muscles so that when the work intensity increases, there will be ample nutrient supply and waste removal.

From week to week and over the course of your base building, the individual workout goals should be to gradually increase mileage and gradually increase pace (or HR) of Breakthrough (BT) workouts. To do that you must again pay attention to periodicity. There are several approaches to the cyclical or periodic nature of base building. The intention is to have one or two building days, followed by one or two recovery days. If we were just cycling or just running, we could probably do a day on/day off or hard day/easy day schedule. But the nature of biathlon training and the benefits of cross-training allow us to occasionally stack hard days (breakthrough days) back to back as in the following scheme:

WEEK 1

SAT: long ride at 65% (BT)

SUN: long run at 70% (BT)

MON: off

TUE: long ride (BT)

WED: long run (BT)

THU: short ride or optional day off (AR)

FRI: short run or optional day off (BE)

Gradually increase both your mileage and your working HR such that by week 6, working HR could be up to 75 percent on the bike and 80 percent running.

First notice that the recommended heart rate (HR) while running is generally 5 percent higher than the riding HR. This translates roughly to 10 beats a minute. The reason for this is that the shock absorption and balance effect of running, absent in cycling, places an additional demand on the musculature and heart, even though our perception of effort might be similar.

Next, look at the pattern of two work days followed either by a complete rest day (off) or two easy days (AR) or (BE). This schedule allows for two possible breakthrough bike rides and two possible breakthrough runs each week. Thursday and Friday here are break-even or active recovery days.

The progression of workload during this type of a base-building strategy would require that each week, over a period of several weeks, you add a mile to the Sunday and Wednesday run and as many as five miles to the Saturday and Tuesday ride. In a progressive-load fashion, you then begin to build a strong base, accumulate some very significant workouts and develop the ability to recover from day to day or week to week. Also note that due to the more disruptive "tear-down" nature of running, it makes sense to do your long ride the day before, rather than the day after your long run. We seem to recover quicker from riding than from running. It also makes sense to plan your day off or an easy bike day after a long run for similar reasons.

In another example of periodization, you might alternate one week of predominantly running with one week of mostly cycling, with the intention that the focus on one allows for greater recovery from the other. In this scenario, the distances of the key workouts also increase over time. The distances of break-even workouts would increase but not as much.

14 DAY ROTATION

Day   1) long ride at 65% (BT)

2) easy short run at 70% (BE)

3) long ride (BT)

4) easy short run (BE)

5) long ride (BT)

6) easy short run (BE)

7) long ride (BT)

8) long run at 70% (BT)

9) day off

10) long run (BT)

11) short ride at 70% (AR)

12) long run (BT)

13) short ride

BASE PHASE BREAKTHROUGH WORKOUTS (BT)

Long rides at 65 - 80 percent MAX HR. Generally flat or rolling terrain. Warm up for the first four or five miles before gradually moving into the target HR for the workout. Steady pacing and steady effort are the main focus. Work on technique (Chapter 8.)

Long runs at 70 - 85 percent MAX HR. Same idea as the rides. Ease into the run with a light jog of a mile or two before working the HR up toward target.Warm down with an easy jog for the final fewminutes.

WEIGHT-TRAINING DURING BASE PHASE

Toward the middle of your base period, you should begin to incorporate a general weight-training program two days a week to prepare for the demands that will soon be placed on legs and arms in the next phases of your training. Endurance training has been shown to reduce strength, but strength remains an important component of speed. Therefore, leg speed and your ability to hold pace can be greatly enhanced by a few well-chosen exercises. Very often I find that sheer strength ultimately becomes the limiting factor for endurance athletes, since cross-training does such a great job of training the cardiovascular system. And upper-body strength can contribute substantially to your maintaining form at the end of long races.

Twice a week seems optimum for biathletes in training because it allows for substantial strength gains without interfering too greatly with your other training recovery requirements. The best time to weight train is after your last ride or run of the day on an easy (BE or AR) day, or on a day off. This way, if you do each set to "exhaustion," you don't have to be concerned about having enough energy left for the roads. Warm up a little before and after each session so as not to pull any muscles. Some people like to stretch lightly between sets while awaiting the next turn. Pay attention to flexibility. Remember that range of motion is as important to speed as strength is.

For most of these exercises you should choose a weight that you can perform 10-12 repetitions per set to start with. As you become stronger and are able to do more than 15 reps, increase the weight. Any more than 15 reps and we begin to leave the realm of anaerobic strength training and re-enter that familiar area of aerobic work. Save that for the roads. Three sets of each exercise should be sufficient, pausing for a short recovery of one to two minutes between each set.

1) BENCH PRESS - Free weights are best; a wider grip is most beneficial to biathletes.

2) LATERAL RAISES - Excellent deltoid exercise for developing power and stamina in the arm-swing. I prefer free-weight dumbbells, but Nautilus, Paramount and Kaiser make some fine lateral-raise machines.

3) LAT PULLDOWNS - For upper back and latisimus dorsi

4) BICEPS CURLS - Whether you use a curling bar or single dumbbells, biceps curls contribute strength to maintain a good 90 degree arm-swing position for the run.

5) PARALLEL BAR DIPS - A great chest, shoulder and triceps combination. Do three sets of as many as you can.

6) QUAD EXTENSIONS - Great for developing strong and injury-free knees, and the kind of quad and thigh strength necessary for hill running and cycling.

7) HAMSTRING CURLS - Very important! The hamstrings are the most neglected running muscles and need to be worked to keep a balance in the musculature of the leg.

8) CALF RAISES - Holding a weight in your hands or standing under a calf machine, rise up and down on your toes, getting a full flex from the calf. This is where that extra inch per stride or one less geartooth per RPM can come from.

9) ABDOMINAL SETS - Any combination of leg lifts, crunches, inclined twisting sit-ups or hanging leg raises will do. Strong abdominals keep the strain off the lower back towards the end of a long run. Ab sets can be done daily, if you are so inclined.

Start this program when there are four weeks left in your base training phase and continue it all the way through the strength phase of the plan.

6

THE STRENGTH PHASE

Maximizing Aerobic Capacity

I call the next major phase of training strength building. The primary goals here are to work on raising your maximum aerobic capacity (VO2 MAX), as well as your anaerobic threshold (AT) and your ability to sustain a high level of work output for long periods of time. During this time it is also important to maximize muscle strength in your weight training program so that it can be applied SPECIFICALLY to your work on the roads. (Translation: speed.) One of the ways VO2 MAX, AT and weight training come together here is in terms of fiber "recruitment." Much of the work in this phase is geared toward involving many previously "unused" muscle fibers to share the loads. This strength phase should last six to eight weeks, depending on your previous experience and the progressive increase in fitness as measured by an occasional time trial or "C" list race.

During the build-up phase, one of the long runs and one of the long rides gets dropped out and an interval or a tempo workout in each event takes its place. The intervals here are high end aerobic training, usually at 85-95 percent MAX HR, and should be of several minutes in duration with similar length rest/recovery intervals. Break-even days will now be a little more subject to change, depending on just how hard you work on the breakthrough days and what sort of recovery pattern you are beginning to see emerge. Always remember that it only takes one or two really great workouts a week to put you way ahead of the game, IF you allow adequate recovery to build from them. Bear in mind also, that once your base has been established, it will stay with you for the entire season, even though you may not be doing as many long rides or runs. It is the intensity of the new work that retains and builds upon your base.

Also during this phase of training, we begin to incorporate the "brick" workout. A brick is a long, steady-paced ride, followed immediately (less than 10 minutes) by a medium-length run. It is, in my opinion, the cornerstone of the biathlon training program. The benefits are several:

● muscle fiber recruitment

● the basic neuromuscular adaptation of going from riding to running

● the "cross-training" benefit of going into a run partially glycogen-depleted (but not necessarily beat up from having already run 10 or 15 miles to reach that state)

● experience in dealing with "the wall" (that point where glycogen reserves are very low and fat metabolism has not yet fully taken over)

● the mental confidence gained from pushing hard on the bike and knowing that there will still be something left for the run

● actual experience with race transition logistics

● a chance to begin to experiment with pacing and the level of workloads you will be capable of handling during races.

After several brick workouts you will notice that what at first felt unfamiliar and uncomfortable soon begins to feel normal and almost routine. It is a great sensation to be at the end of a long hard bike ride and actually be looking forward to the run rather than dreading it.

Examples of strength phase training weeks:

14 DAY ROTATION:

Day   1) long hill ride at 80 - 85% MAX HR (BT)

2) long hill run at 80 - 85% MAX HR (BT)

3) off

4) a.m. time trial ride (BT)
p.m. run easy 6 mile (AR)

5) ride 20 (BE)

6) a.m. ride 20 easy (AR)
p.m. interval run 5 x 1 mile at 85 - 95% (BT)

7) off

8) brick (BT)

9) ride 15 (AR)

10) a.m. ride 20 easy (BE)
p.m. run 4 easy

11) a.m. run easy
p.m. ride hill repeats (BT)

12) run 8-10 at 80% (BE)

13) a.m. running hill repeats (BT)
   p.m. ride 20 easy (AR)

14) run 5 or ride 15 (BE)

Notice that in this schedule there are seven Break-through sessions (BT), four Break-even (BE) and three complete days of either Active Rest (AR) or days off. A more detailed description of individual workouts follows. The schedule repeats itself every 14 days. As a blend of specific workouts, it contains one brick, one long run, one long ride, one aerobic cycling interval session, one cycle time trial and two aerobic running interval sessions. It builds upon the base we have established and pushes AT and VO2 MAX higher. The weekly mileage might be considered low, but there is plenty of work and adequate rest in this schedule. Although the mileage and loads will vary for each athlete, it is the relative placement of work sessions and rest sessions that is the key here. You are the coach, and any specific (BT) workouts you feel you need can be substituted for (BT)s on this list.

Progression of workload over repeating 14-day segments can come from two options. The first - extend the mileage of long runs or rides, or do additional numbers of intervals at the same working HR. For example, you could add four miles to your brick ride and a mile to your brick run every time you do that workout, keeping your working HR constant at the lower end of your training range until you are able to complete a 40 or 50 mile ride followed by a 6 mile run. The second option - once you have hit some good single-workout mileage peaks and have arrived at maximum numbers of intervals, hold those numbers constant and gradually increase the average working HR for each session. In so doing, you will automatically be increasing your speed. Time trial distances would stay constant, but you would intend to lower your personal best on the same course each time you went out to do it.

SAMPLE 7 DAY ROTATION

Day 1) brick (BT)

2) ride 15 (AR)

3) run 8-10 medium (BE)

4) a.m. time trial bike ride or ride hill repeats (BT)
p.m. run 6 easy

5) medium length easy ride (BE)

6) a.m. track intervals or running hill repeats (BT)
p.m. easy ride

7) easy ride or easy run (BE)

The seven-day rotation contains three (BT)s, which should be more than enough to assure a progressive increase in fitness. I suggest that you occasionally substitute other breakthrough workouts from the following list to make sure that you are addressing every goal of this training phase and to simply keep the workouts exciting and fresh.

STRENGTH PHASE BREAKTHROUGH WORKOUTS

Long steady rides at 80-85 percent. Same as in base phase but with a slight increase in intensity. Work towards increasing both intensity and distance. For beginners, 40 miles is a good maximum to work up to. For elite, anything up to 100. Training distances over 100 miles has little value for biathlon racing.

Long steady runs at 85-90 percent. Same as the rides, except eight miles is a good beginner max, 12 intermediate, 20 for elites.

Long hill rides. This is a form of interval training, except that it is a continuous ride. To begin to work leg strength, some rides will now be in the hills (if hills are available). Keep the heart monitor on and allow the HR to run up to 90 or 95 percent during longer climbs and let it back off to below the target range for recovery on the downhills.

Long hill runs. Similar to the ride. Work hard on the ascents and cruise the descents.

Riding hill repeats. An interval session of between three and eight minutes duration. Pick a hill with a 6-8 percent grade and after a five-mile warm-up, climb the hill at 85-95 percent HR. Do not exceed 95 percent for now. Stay seated during the climb. Work from the outer hips, butt and upper thighs. When you reach the top of the hill, record your time, immediately turn around and coast back down. That is your rest interval. Upon reaching the bottom, go again. Repeat as many intervals as the schedule calls for. Beginners start with two or three. Elites work up to doing six on a good day.

Running hill repeats. Similar to riding. Choose a 300 to 800-meter hill and after a two-mile warm-up run, do anywhere from six to 10 depending on fitness and the length of your hill, at 85 - 95 percent and up to 100 percent HR. Work on stride power by emphasizing the arm-swing and the push off the rear foot (see chapter 8 on technique). Warm down.

Track Intervals. Measured on the track to give you some indication of an accurate pace per mile, these are interval sessions of one to two miles. Nothing shorter yet. 85 - 95 percent HR. Do a half-mile walk/jog recovery in between, but be sure your HR comes down to your resting plateau before beginning the next work interval. Do anywhere from three to six if doing repeat miles, two to four if doing repeat deuces (two milers). Start with what you feel is about 10k race pace.

Cycling Intervals. Find a flat stretch with little or no traffic if possible. Use your cyclocomputer, if you have one, to measure off distances on the bike. Warm up with five to 10 miles, then do several two to four-mile work intervals at 85 - 95 percent, staying seated all the way. Spin easy during the rest interval for the duration of your work interval.

Heart Monitor Road Running Intervals. (Also called Tempo Runs.) Based on time rather than distance. Using your monitor and watch, hold anywhere from 90 - 100 percent HR for time. Five to 10-minute work intervals are best. The great thing here is that you don't need a track because exact distance is not important. Time spent at or near VO2 MAX is the key. Always warm up before and warm down afterwards.

Brick Intervals - A variation on the brick is the brick interval, which is series of controlled cycling and running intervals done at the running track with a stationary bike or wind trainer very close by. Start with an easy warm up on the bike, then go 10 minutes hard on the bike (85 percent), dismount immediately, change shoes and run one mile at 90 percent. When you finish the mile, change again and hop right back on the bike, repeating the ride/run sequence. The transition becomes your rest interval. These will give you the very specific neuromuscular patterning and fiber recruitment to handle ride/run transitions as well as the experience of an interval workout that is actually continuous. Some fibers will get a chance to recover while others right next to them go to work. Beginners do three sets of ride/run. Elites work up to six all out.

7

THE SPEED PHASE

The Finishing Touches

The final working phase of training leading up to your first racing peak is called the speed phase. By now, the long-distance work and the high-end aerobic work in interval and tempo sessions should have you at or nearly at your highest potential aerobic capacity (VO2 MAX). Equally as important, your anaerobic threshold (AT) will have risen substantially, so that you are able to perform at a high heart rate for long periods of time. The speed phase is designed to put the finishing touches on your racing fitness by increasing your lactate tolerance. You will recall that after maximizing VO2 and AT, the next most significant barrier to peak performance is your ability to tolerate and recycle the increasing amounts of lactates you will be producing when you race at the higher end of your AT. By occasionally doing intervals that exceed 100 percent MAX HR, you will now be training your body to recognize and withstand the fatigue associated with the highest sustainable work output during races, to handle and reprocess increasing amounts of lactates (you are only able to do this so well now by virtue of your base and strength work), and to maximize the last component of speed; leg-turnover.

As a rule, your overall mileage might fall slightly during this phase, but the intensity of the individual BT workouts will increase. The long ride and long run done either singularly or as a brick stay on the schedule and the working heart rate for those workouts will increase a few BPMs. Some of what were high-end aerobic intervals now become anaerobic or supermax intervals. Where once you might have done five or six repeat miles at 90 percent HR, you may now do three or four at heart rates that approach or exceed 100 percent MAX HR during the second half-mile. Some shorter intervals like quarters and halves are now recommended at a nearly all-out pace and with minimal recovery time between.

Cycling workouts are similar. Shorter hill-climb repeats at all-out pace, all-out time trials, and all-out brick intervals are the key Breakthrough workouts during this phase. As in the previous phases, we're not talking about a lot of workouts of this nature - one running, one cycling and perhaps one combination per week is plenty. Fill the gaps with your one or two long sessions and some easy BE workouts. Several weeks of this kind of focus, and suddenly, maintaining your anaerobic threshold will seem infinitely more comfortable.

SAMPLE SPEED PHASE 14-DAY ROTATION:

Day   1) brick at 85-95% MAX HR (BT)

       2) ride 20 (AR)

       3) a.m. run 7 (BE)
          p.m. ride 20

       4) a.m. ride 20
          p.m. interval run 12 x 400 at 100-105% HR (BT)

       5) off

       6) a.m. ride hill sprints (BT)
          p.m. run easy 7

7) a.m. ride 20, run 4 (BE)

8) brick intervals (BT)

9) long ride at 80-85% (BE)

10) easy 20 spin (AR)

11) long run from 8 - 16 at 80-85% (BE)

12) time trial ride 10 miles at 100%, run 4 (BT)

13) a.m. run track intervals 3x1 mile at
     100% (BT)
     p.m. ride 20 easy

14) off

This particular schedule has six breakthrough sessions (BT), four break-even (BE), two active recovery (AR) and two days off, spaced well enough apart that you should benefit from each. Any number of variations on this rotation can work. As before, substitute some other BT workouts where you see it necessary to be even more specific, or where it may be more convenient. Also, "B" and "C" list races may be substituted for weekend workouts if you feel ready. Record times and, where possible, heart rates of intervals, time trials and races in your log the day you do them. Check on fitness once a week by doing a submax test as a warm-up before hard interval workouts. As always, when in doubt about your recovery, take an AR day or a day off.

As BT workouts start to repeat themselves every 14 days, try to bring your interval times down a few seconds and shave more time off the time trials. These and your "C" and "B" list races are your milestones. It is not absolutely critical that your times always fall; sometimes weather conditions may slow you down or you might just have an off day. But over time, you should be noticing improvement. If for some reason you are not, take an objective look at your schedule and make sure you are not overtraining. Do a submax test to be certain. At this time of the season, overtraining can have disastrous results. My short-term cure for a mild case of overtraining is two days off followed by three BE days, then pick up the regular schedule again.

An alternative to this 14-day example is a seven-day schedule that allows you to input BT workouts and "C" list races while maintaining a generally consistent plan of action. Those who work regular hours often find a seven-day rotation fits their schedule a little better.

SAMPLE SPEED PHASE 7-DAY ROTATION:

Day　1)　spin 20 (AR) or off

2)　a.m. run 10 (BE)
　　p.m. ride 20

3)　a.m. sub max warm-up then run track
　　intervals 800's or miles (BT)
　　p.m. ride 15

4)　ride 40 at 80-85% (BE)

5)　a.m. ride hill repeats or time trial or brick
　　intervals (BT)
　　p.m. run 4 - 6

6)　a.m. run 7 (BE)
　　p.m. ride 10

7)　brick or "B" or "C" list race

SPEED PHASE BREAKTHROUGH WORKOUTS

Brick intervals - Same as in strength phase but more intense. Warm up 10 or 15 minutes on the bike, then go 10 minutes hard (90-95 percent) on the bike, get off, change shoes quickly and do your mile at 95 per cent or better. Repeat. Three complete ride/run sequences is enough, five is max for elites.

Short track intervals - 400's or 800's. Two-mile easy warm-up, then do five or six accelerating 100's to get the turnover going. If you choose to do 400's, do them all-out and give yourself a 200-meter walk/jog rest. Eight is minimum, 16 maximum for elites. If 800's, do them at 95 percent or better and keep a 400-meter rest interval. Four for beginners, eight as a max figure for elites.

Cycling hill sprints - 8-12 percent grade this time. Half-mile up to a mile distance is best. Warm up with five to 10 miles first, then sprint all-out to the top, alternating one interval sitting with one standing up this time. Six for beginners, up to 12 for elites. Take a good 15-mile spin-down afterwards.

Bike time trial - After a solid 10 - 15-mile warm-up, time trial a 10-mile course all-out (90 percent or better). Spin 10 miles after. For elites, a tough variation is warm up five, time trial 10-20, spin 10 and time trial back 10-20. Warm down.

Running time trial or tempo run - Pick a course from three to six miles and after a two-mile gradual warm-up, time trial the course. Wearing a heart monitor is best, because the goal is to maintain as close to 95 percent HR as possible. Warm down with 2 miles.

Running repeat miles - Two-mile warm up, then three x one mile at 95 percent or better. Elites do up to five. Two-mile warm down.

Long rides, long runs, bricks - Same as strength phase but at higher heart rates (or maintain same HR but go faster!) For elites, ride mileage should not exceed 100, the run 20, bricks 70 and seven.

"B" or "C" list race - When you feel like it, enter one of the less important races on your schedule as a means of familiarizing yourself with pace, your new fitness, and your new sense of how hard you can actually go without hitting the wall.

Motorpacing and paceline riding - For Elites only. These can be quite dangerous and require expert bike handling skills. Motorpacing is basically drafting behind a motorcycle in a controlled workout situation. It can simulate the speeds, high turnover (RPMs), and anaerobic threshold work you will encounter during a race (although drafting is illegal in biathlon races). Riding in a controlled paceline can also be great interval training, provided you can get to the front often enough to take your anaerobic pulls. In both cases, since you are often at the mercy of the person in front of you, I don't recommend this as your optimum form of training. Nor is it something you should do on a frequent basis.

8

FORM AND FUNCTION

CYCLING TECHNIQUE

Your goal during the ride portion of any biathlon should be fairly obvious: to cover ground as quickly as possible and still have something left to complete the second run if there is one. Therein lies a dilemma. Expend too much energy during the ride and the two minutes you pick up may cost you five during the run. On the other hand, even a moderately hard ride will affect your run time, so why not pick up as much on the bike as possible? Your cycling technique will play a large part in maximizing speed in both the ride and the run, thereby solving the dilemma.

The most important aspect of biathlon cycling is what I call controlled relaxation. Rather than flailing away with every part of your body in an effort to expend the most energy possible, try to confine all output to the hips, thighs and calves. Leave the arms, neck, shoulders and back out of it. Consciously relax those upper body parts while focusing all your drive and energy from the waist down. Even during extreme climbing, when you find yourself out of the saddle, it is crucial to relax your upper body.

Most biathletes use some form of aerodynamic handlebars. Not only do these bars reduce wind resistance, they actually allow you to rest your back, arms, neck and shoulders while you focus the work on the legs. A proper setup on "aero" bars will allow you to get a full extension in the legs without rocking your hips, and will give you a flat or slightly rounded back without your head slumping between your shoulders. It is this posture that you will assume for the majority of training rides and races.

When you are in an aero position, cadence should be anywhere from 75 to 100 rpms. Any slower or faster and you probably need another gear. During early season, higher rpms in a lower gear are best. Later, as your strength increases, you may find it more economical to push a higher gear at lower rpms. Whatever your choice of gearing, make sure that you are not bouncing (rpms too high) or struggling (rpms too low, gear too tough). Remember, isolate the lower half of the body and do all the work with it. Someone riding next to you should not be able to see your head waggle, your shoulders sway or your back move.

Your breathing should be rhythmic and not constrained by your position on the bike. As in running, the active part of breathing is the exhalation. Exhale fully and just let the air fall into the lungs. It is not necessary nor recommended to try to fill the lungs full of air. Two-thirds of a lung full is more than adequate, easy to accomplish passively, and contributes more to a controlled relaxation. The frequency of your breathing will obviously be determined by the work load.

The primary work in cycling is done specifically by the gluteus, the rectus femoris, the vastus lateralis, and the quadriceps (the butt, the outer thigh and the quads). Think of each stroke as a piston push emanating from the butt and moving down the leg. As you push that piston down, pull the opposite piston up with the hamstrings and illiopsoas (top front of thigh).

The calf muscle is an important part of the transmission of all this power to the pedals. Thus, it seems much more efficient to limit the degree of flexion and extension occurring at the foot during each stroke. Flexion manifests itself as dipping the heels below the pedal at the bottom of the stroke. In some ways this can be seen as a shock absorber that reduces the force coming from the thigh to the pedal, when what we want is actually FULL FORCE being transmitted. Therefore, maintaining a slight extension (toe pointed slightly down), with maybe an inch of leeway (or flex) would be ideal foot placement. Remember also that too much flexion/extension movement will unnecessarily tire the lower legs and interfere with the run.

The normal posture on the seat can be altered slightly for short portions of hill climbs or headwinds. During these more intense efforts, slide back an inch or two on the saddle and bring your hands back towards you on the bars. With regular bars, both the crossbar and the brake hoods are good positions. With aero bars, find a hand placement that accommodates your new position in the saddle and allows you to sit up just a little more. Power transmission through the legs remains the same.

Occasionally, it will be necessary or convenient to stand up while riding. Accelerating out of a corner or climbing steep sections of hill are such times. It's a matter of personal preference, but some biathletes find it easier to remain standing during a lengthy climb. Once again the key is to relax. Maintain a firm grip on the widest part of your handlebars and let the bike sway from side to side underneath you as you apply extra weight to the pedals while standing upright. Keep the wheels moving in a straight line on the road, not weaving in and out. As you apply pressure to the pedal, pull up with just the fingers (not the whole arm) on the handlebar on the same side. Find a rhythm to let the bike go easily from side to side. Don't wiggle your butt or snake your back to accomplish this. Keep the body relaxed and over the continuous centerline of the bike. In other words, move the bike side to side, not your body. Avoid leaning into the front of your bike. If anything, hang your butt slightly out the back so that the front of the seat almost touches the back of your thigh when the bike moves under you.

As is often the case in endurance events, finding your rhythm is a key to efficient (fast) cycling. Breathing, cadence and controlled relaxation of the upper body establishes a rhythm which will enable you to focus your energy on covering the most ground in the least amount of time. Whether on workouts or in races, notice the rhythm that you set up for yourself and use it as a focus for the work you are doing.

Descending doesn't require a great deal of aerobic work work, but it does demand some technique and your total focus. It is hardly worth taking reckless chances while descending to gain a few seconds here or there, when those seconds can be easily made up in the first few hundred meters of the next climb or flat stretch. The risk of a crash is too great. Whether training or racing, never descend faster than your skills can handle. Brake adequately before entering corners, not while halfway through them. Keep the inside pedal high on tight turns and don't start pedaling out of a turn until you are upright enough to allow your pedals to clear the pavement. The longer crankarms you have, the more upright you need to be before resuming pedaling.

RUNNING TECHNIQUE

All too often, biathletes choose to go out too hard on the first run or the ride and then just hang on in the final run. Form starts to fall apart during that last run as glycogen reserves are depleted and dehydration takes its toll. Suddenly, all kinds of compromises in form are made such as overstriding, rolling the shoulders, dropping the head and arms and completely losing rhythm. As a result, speed goes down the tubes. However, the truth is that no matter how tired you are, if you can maintain form you will run faster.

The secret to developing and maintaining efficient running form is to temporarily become a 400-meter runner when you are on the track, and a miler when you are on the roads. This will help you run like a 10k runner in a biathlon. Actually visualize the form and grace of a world-class middle-distance runner and you will seem to become one. By focusing on technique at the track, you can let those elements shape your road-running style.

The most important component of track running posture is the head position. Think "proud." The head is held relatively high, with the chin up slightly so that a neutral (eyes straight ahead) gaze would be fixed on the horizon. This proud posture automatically opens the chest up a little, making breathing easier. The shoulders should follow suit, up and back slightly, but relaxed. As in cycling, let the air fall into your lungs passively and make the exhalation more forceful.

Next, the hips should be as far forward as is comfortable to ensure a good extension off the rear foot. The arms should be close to a 90-degree angle at the elbow with the hands held in a loose fist, or at the very least, slightly open but not flopping.

The action of the arm-swing on the track approaches a straight-forward/straight-back movement the faster you go. Conversely, the slower you are running, the more the arm-swing will tend to go side to side. Technically and biomechanically, this is inefficient. Sprint drills and hill running reinforce the benefits of keeping the motion in as forward a line as possible. If you work on this at the track, some of that forward motion will stay with you on the roads.

A common mistake biathletes make in exaggerating arm-swing at first is to push the arm forward as if reaching for something. Actually, the key to effective arm-swing is to actively draw the arm back at the elbow as if to cock it and then let it fall forward. This keeps the shoulders back and high in that proud position. It also allows you to effectively dictate your leg turnover with your arms, a useful skill when the legs are just not willing to get going after a hard ride.

It is also important to bring the knees through high on the track to get a full extension off the rear foot and to maximize stride length without actually overstriding. Overstriding occurs when the foot lands so far in front of you that it actually brakes your speed temporarily. Ideally, your foot should land directly under your hips just as your momentum has carried you through that space. Land on the full foot (for most, this is actually the full outside half), with the major impact absorption and push-off taking place over the ball of the foot.

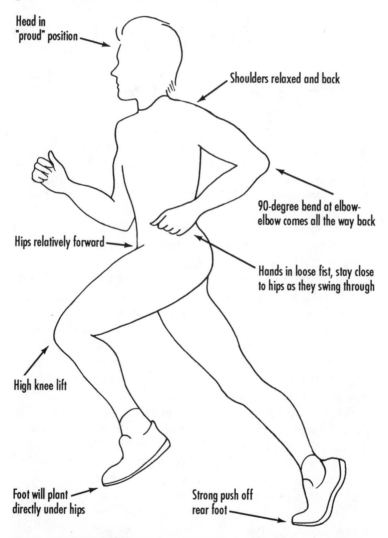

Head in "proud" position

Shoulders relaxed and back

90-degree bend at elbow-elbow comes all the way back

Hips relatively forward

Hands in loose fist, stay close to hips as they swing through

High knee lift

Foot will plant directly under hips

Strong push off rear foot

FIG. 8 GOOD TRACK RUNNING FORM TRANSLATES TO EFFICIENT ROAD RUNNING STYLE.

9

THE TAPER

The Final Steps to Peak Performance

The taper is an extremely important part of your race strategy. A well-planned taper can make a race a complete success. By the same token, a poorly planned or non-existent taper can make your race at best a waste of time and at worst, can set you back several weeks.

The reason for tapering before a race is to give your body time to recover, rest, build and gather strength before the real challenge of a race is mounted. As I noted previously, many of the specific training exercises and workouts we do take a few days to have their total positive training effect (cumulative effects). While we are in a training mode, we may only take one easy day or day off after a hard session, and then jump right back into it the next day not quite fully recovered. This is usually acceptable during training because generally our best efforts in training won't break us down as much as a race will. After all, we are looking to achieve the fastest possible accumulation of positive stresses and rests we can safely handle. The truth, however, is that during this training time we are never fully recovered because our bodies lag a few days behind in responding to the stimuli of each workout. This is what makes us so susceptible to the pitfalls of overtraining. During training, we choose to ride that fine line anyway, knowing we can back off a few days if we need to catch up.

With this idea in mind, it follows then that a brief

period of easy workouts and rest just prior to an important "A" or "B" list race will give us time to totally recover from previous breakthrough workouts and build to a PEAK on the day of a race. Some athletes have a fear that fitness will actually be lost during a taper if they do too little for too long a period of time. This is highly unlikely if you adhere to a few simple guidelines. I have seen some outrageously strong performances follow some extraordinarily long tapers.

For short biathlons and for well-conditioned biathletes, a four or five day taper is optimum. For a longer, say three-or four-hour event, one week of tapering is probably best. I firmly believe that even longer tapers can be beneficial if the proper workload is maintained. It is always better to err on the side of too long a taper rather than too brief, just as I would always prefer to enter a race slightly undertrained as opposed to slightly overtrained.

Another point to keep in mind is that it only takes 50 percent of the work to maintain a level of fitness that it took to achieve that level in the first place. This actually holds true over a period of several weeks, and is a good rule of thumb to fall back on any time you think you might be close to overtraining. In any case, it is reassuring to know that by doing half of the effort or half of the mileage of any workout, you will not lose ANY fitness.

So how much work constitutes an ideal taper? When coming off that final hard week of quality training, make the last day before your taper period a good solid effort, possibly even a breakthrough day. In general, the first day of your taper then becomes a day OFF. The second day of your taper would be a short, break-even workout at very light loads. The following days depend on the length of your chosen taper period, but reserve the day before the race to do no more than 10 easy miles of cycling and two easy miles of running. I would tell you to take it completely off because I think sometimes that total rest is best, but I know how guilty or jumpy most biathletes feel taking that last day off. It's almost as if you need to remind yourself that you still remember how to ride and run since you've had a few easy days in a row and are chomping at the bit.

A final word on the taper. Use this time to actually visualize the strength and power returning to you and coursing through your body. Rest and prepare mentally for the race as well as physically. During that last workout on the day before the race, just sense how ready you are to chew up the course.

SAMPLE TAPER

Day 1) medium brick (BT)

2) off

3) spin 25

4) run 6

5) ride 15

6) run 5

7) ride 10, run 2 very easy

8) RACE

10

THE RACE

Putting it All Together

Y ou're ready. You've trained smart. Now it's time to put yourself to the test. Get out your race list.

When possible, enter races early by mail. That way you will probably get your race number and instructions in advance and have one less thing to worry about race day. If the race is more than an hour's drive away, think seriously about staying at a hotel nearby the night before. Nothing can leave you feeling flatter at the starting line than a two hour drive.

When possible, get your bike checked the day or night before the race. This will give you time to get used to any adjustments the inspecting mechanic might make or suggest. Right, one less thing to worry about race day.

Drive the race course or better yet, ride it on your bike several days before the race. Familiarize yourself with the hills, the descents, the intersections and the mileage markers. Above all, shake hands with it and make it your friend. If it has a tough hill or no shade, remember that everyone has to climb the same hill and run in the same heat.

Attend pre-race meetings. You never know when the weather, city council or the race director has forced an emergency course change.

If you are out of town, make dinner reservations well in advance. Large, late dinners the night before a race are definitely not wise. Eat early and lightly. No alcohol.

On race morning allow plenty of time to eat, get to the race, rack your bike, check in if you haven't already, warm up and go to the bathroom twice.

Eat lightly one-and-a-half to two hours before the race. Maybe a muffin and some tea. Sip water every 20 minutes until race time.

Make sure you have everything you need at the transition area: a towel to stand or sit on, bike and running shoes (some biathletes use two pairs of running shoes for run-bike- run format races so they don't have to untie and re-tie the pair they tore off after the first run), helmet, Vaseline, filled water bottles, any race food loosely wrapped and easily reached, goggles, and any other items you require. Double check.

Go over your race strategy in your mind. Do you know where the one-mile splits are and what times you'll be listening for to be sure you're on pace? Are you certain of the course, the entrances to and exits from transition areas?

If you have time, spin the bike a mile or two as a warmup and equipment check, re-rack it, making sure it is in the gear you will want to take off in, and then jog a half mile or so. As race time approaches, do a series of gradually accelerating 100-meter shake-ups. Five or six is good. Actually get a little lactic acid forming and recycling. Then jog easily another half mile. As a result, when the gun goes off you should shift fairly quickly into fat metabolism, provided you don't take off too fast. Without this type of warm-up, the body immediately goes anaerobic for a short while and you spend the next few miles trying to recycle an abundance of lactic acid while maintaining an otherwise aerobic pace. This way, you beat it to the punch and stay aerobic earlier and longer.

To avoid taking off too fast or slow, line up at the starting line with people your speed. If you're too close to the front, you'll get stomped on. Too far back and you'll lose time as you do the stomping. Don't hesitate to ask what pace those around you intend to run.

Make sure your watch is set at 00. Start it as the gun goes off and then settle into your pace as soon as you possibly can. It is always better to go out a little slow rather than too fast. If you're wearing a heart monitor, stick with your working race HR numbers but allow yourself some time to reach target. If you reach your target HR level before the first mile, you are probably working too hard. Just settle in during that first run, work but enjoy it, and always back off when you feel the pace quickening. Run your race, not the other athlete's.

As you approach the transition area, stay calm and focused. Know exactly the order in which you will remove running shoes, don bike shoes and helmet, unrack the bike and take off. Start the first half-mile at a moderate - not all out - pace. Just because you are warmed up from the run doesn't mean your specific cycling muscle fibers are quite ready to hammer away on the bike. Allow the heart rate to increase gradually over the first mile or three until it reaches target. If your race is destined to last more than two hours, start to consume your first fuel a mile or two into the bike. This way it will start to kick in around mile 10 or 15. Drink fluids as you have trained, a minimum of six ounces every half-hour. Always think a half-hour in advance when eating and drinking during long races.

Find your rhythm in your breathing and cadence. Focus your vision on the road 100 meters ahead. Be aware of peripheral surroundings but maintain that focal point as you reel in the riders ahead of you. As you pass them, maintain form and rhythm and silently thank them for contributing to your energy and speed.

The last mile of the ride, shift to a gear easier than you ordinarily would ride and spin a little to prepare for the final run. As you enter the bike-to-run transition, slow down and focus on the task ahead. Be certain you follow the racking procedure with your bike. Remove your helmet and put your running shoes on calmly, avoiding any frantic pulling which by now could be fatal to your already exhausted and cramp-prone muscles.

Head out on the run and immediately begin to find

that rhythm. Easy for me to say, right? The key to the second run is to actually develop the same leg turnover you had in the first run, but shorten the stride length. The biggest mistake is overstriding in a desperate attempt to compensate for the fatigue setting in and lack of speed. If you can hold it together, maintain form and turnover and just allow the stride length to stay short, you will immediately begin to pick people off even as you are "warming up." Then as the legs begin to work again, allow the stride to lengthen when you feel comfortable. Pace that final run so that you know you can hold pace right to the finish.

Maintaining focus becomes critical now as everything begins to feel like it is falling apart. This is the time to get into the "Zone," a Zen-like state of mind where all those loud random thoughts of pain, fatigue and paranoia give way to a calm sense of inner focus. It is, after all, the mind that ultimately controls the pace here. And rhythm is the key to reaching the "ZONE."

All the work you did on the track is now coming to your aid. Arm-swing stays steady and rhythmic like a metronome and actually dictates your leg turnover. Keep your gaze focused on the road 40 yards in front of you and just notice your hands entering and leaving your visual periphery. Now focus your hearing on just the sounds of your breathing and your footfall. Relax the muscles in your face and let the tension out of your neck and shoulders. You'll begin to feel a sense of control and calm. Awareness of fatigue and pain may come and go but they are now more just bits of information to make minor adjustments in stride or rhythm than subjective or emotional thoughts about stopping. If you have done any of the visualization processes (chapter 12), now is the time to utilize them.

If those thoughts about stopping do persist, allow yourself two crisis situations and two "magic bullets" to deal with them. A crisis can be stomach cramps, a stitch, nausea, plain-old abject fatigue or any situation that threatens to take your race away. Magic bullets are a change of pace or rhythm, usually faster than you are currently doing, which temporarily abate the crisis by altering the neuromuscular frequency. Yes, believe it or not, some-times just picking up the pace for a short distance can get rid of a stitch, that wave of nausea or that feeling of gastric distress. But it is risky to approach a crisis so aggressively, and two magic bullets are about all you can realistically hope for in any one race. Otherwise, try to stay in the "ZONE" as much as you can.

As the finish line draws near, increase your pace to the extent that you can and finish strong. Don't forget to stop your watch. Sometimes race results and times aren't available for weeks. Record that time and any splits and heart rates you can remember while they are fresh in your mind. Now go and enjoy the post-race festivities.

During the next few days, analyze your race. Did you fulfill any of the goals you listed in chapter 4 of this program? Did you follow a master plan, and do you feel you gave it all you had? Did you hold form, or did technique fall apart? Was the strength there but no endur-ance? Did you eat and drink enough before and during the race? Did you hold focus? Record your analysis in your log, and begin to look for weaknesses that need work. Over the next few weeks, after full recovery, choose break-through workouts that will specifically strengthen those weaknesses.

11

RACE RECOVERY TRAINING

Maintaining That Peak

The days after a race also require some strategic planning so that your recovery will be maximized. Without adequate recovery from racing, your ability to resume training and competing are in serious jeopardy. Remember that a race is a confrontation with the both race course and yourself. It should be a supreme effort. If you raced well, you probably did some minor damage at both the micro (cellular) and the macro (muscle, tendon, ligament) levels. This is normal and nothing to worry about. However, the harder you raced and the longer the course was, the longer your recovery period is likely to be.

The irony is that for most athletes, the harder you run, the better you feel (except for the general soreness and stiffness) and based on great race results, you can't wait to resume training. This can be a big mistake and, in fact, costs many good athletes valuable time during the season. Somehow, the brain and the body get separated after a race. The brain decides that the body did so well in the last race, that its going to train even harder for the next one - starting today. In truth, some long biathlons take weeks to recover from before serious training can resume. Most of the time, however, a good week of recovery training is best to put you back in the proper physical state to resume a normal workload.

To simplify, a recovery training period should almost look like the reverse of a taper. The day after a race, it is probably best to do an easy spin on the bike of no more than 10 miles at such a low heart rate that your friends would laugh at you. Maybe 100 beats a minute maximum. This is entirely a therapy ride (active recovery) designed to decrease muscle stiffness and allow a little blood to flow through the legs and remove waste products. The second day after a race, do another easy ride and a short easy (very easy) jog. If your biathlon was really short, the third day you can work up to a break-even day; if it was longer, another easy short ride and/or run combination. I emphasize that you will probably feel great and ready to roll full-speed again. Trust that your body is probably still not ready, that it is only your ego telling you to hurry up and work harder. Patience is a virtue here and, as is usually the case with endurance training, it pays to take another day off when in doubt.

At any time during this week, preferably sooner, get a professional massage if you can. Aside from the fact that it just feels great and you probably deserve it, a sports massage will also speed recovery by flushing even more of those race toxins into the blood stream, through the lymph nodes and out of the body.

After a week or more of easing back into the program, after all stiffness from the race has disappeared, you may now resume training at your pre-taper level.

If your next race is soon, be sure to schedule your building work to allow for the same tapering process as your recent race. By the way, did that amount of tapering time work well for you? If not, make any adjustments now and put them into your schedule.

When races are scheduled fairly close together, sometimes the best we can do after recovery-training, is to throw one or two good breakthrough workouts in, maybe some 95-100 percent work on the track or some 90 percent 20-minute bike interval sessions. That will be more than sufficient if you remember that you probably helped increase your fitness in the race (as long as you recovered properly!) and you are now at a near peak level. Maintenance and avoiding injury are the primary goals between races. Increasing fitness is the secondary goal.

If your next race is several weeks away, begin to build again with some high-end aerobic work similar to the last weeks of your strength phase, then proceed to the speed phase for the final few weeks before tapering. Repeat this process as races appear on your schedule.

12

SPARE PARTS

The Other Elements

DIET

One of the key factors in determining the effectiveness of your training is diet. The nutritional part of your recovery is as important as rest. You are out there hammering and stressing yourself several times a week. It makes no sense to tear yourself down and then not provide adequate materials to rebuild and benefit from all that work. Muscles operate on fuel just as any engine does, and the higher octane the fuel, the better the engine performs.

First a word on fats. Much has been written on the subject of fats over the past 10 years and most of it has been negative. The typical high-fat American diet has been shown to contribute to heart disease, obesity, cancer and just plain lethargy. Yet it is interesting to note that fats play a major part in the endurance athlete's ability to perform at high levels over long periods of time. The burning of free fatty acids at a high rate is what allows the athlete to spare precious glycogen. As you will recall, when glycogen is depleted, the ball game is basically over. This ability to burn fats is of major significance to the endurance athlete. Much of our training time focuses on developing that ability. The irony is that the better we become at burning fats, the more we tap into the stored fats we carry around with us until

our body-fat levels are ridiculously low. If we are sup-
posed to avoid dietary fats, where do we get these free fatty
acids so crucial to avoiding glycogen depletion?   The
answer is that virtually everything we consume can be
converted to fats. Protein that is not used for repair or
growth, and carbohydrate not stored as glycogen can be
converted to either free fatty acids or stored fat. So we need
not be concerned with getting enough fat in our diet. In
fact, our concern should continue to focus on avoiding
dietary fat. Note also that because fat is so efficient a fuel,
a 150 pound biathlete who has six percent bodyfat (very
low) has enough stored fat to theoretically walk/run 90
miles and still have 2/3 of his fat stores left!

Complex carbohydrates should supply the bulk of
your training diet. Grains, pasta, whole-wheat breads and
muffins, potatoes, rice, beans and green vegetables are all
excellent sources of complex carbs.   Most world-class
biathletes and triathletes subsist on a diet made up exclu-
sively of these foods. The less processed and preservative-
laden you can find them, the better. Fully 80 percent of
your caloric intake should come from these foods.

Due to some very outdated information, athletes are
often unnecessarily concerned about whether they are
getting enough protein. Protein is absolutely essential to
the rebuilding process, but athletes can make a big mistake
in taking in too much protein. According to recent data,
one gram of protein per kilogram of bodyweight should be
plenty to make all the necessary repairs. This would work
out to a little more than one small can of tuna fish per day
for the average person if that person ate nothing else. In
fact, the complex carbohydrate diet mentioned above contains more than enough protein in and of itself (without
any supplementation of meat or fish), provided you vary
the ingredients and consume enough calories. This brings
up the often heated discussion of whether you are better off
as a vegetarian or supplementing with meats. Ultimately,
it is only a matter of personal preference. There is no
definitive right or wrong approach. If you are smart about
your choice and amount of foods, the vegetarian approach

works well. If, on the other hand, you feel the need to supplement with lean red meats, chicken or fish, do so, but bear in mind that portions are best kept small (less than 4 ounces at a time). Experiment with both ways and go with whichever works best for you. Just do as much as you can to avoid animal fats. Also, keep dairy products to a minimum, since they are usually higher in fats and we have no real requirements for them after adolescence.

As for simple sugars, fruits, sweets, etc., I find these to be excellent sources of immediate energy during the day. Some people argue that simple sugars create a roller-coaster effect with insulin levels and therefore cause either very high or very low blood-sugar levels. I think that the better trained you are, the more your body will tend to store these immediately as glycogen and blood glucose. With that in mind, I like to confine my intake of simple sugars to just after or just before a workout.

The use or avoidance of alcohol has been the subject of debate among athletes for years. Provided you are not an abuser, I see little wrong with an occasional beer or glass of wine. Many top biathletes consume vast quantities of the amber nectar. Beer does contain some rather healthy ingredients such as hops, barley and other grains. I personally drink a non-alcoholic beer the way friends of mine drink juice or water. As for wine, I recommend staying away from red wine the night before a race or a (BT) workout. The histamines in wine cause a mild allergic reaction which affects the diameter of the blood vessels for several hours, resulting in anything from headaches to just general tiredness. Also be aware that alcohol in any form has a dehydrating effect.

So many extraordinary biochemical changes are occurring daily in the body of a training biathlete that it is probably wise to take some simple form of multi-vitamin/multi-mineral supplement as insurance. I recommend this because, unfortunately, we can't trust that the foods we purchase in the supermarket will provide all the necessary trace nutrients we require. I do not, however, recommend protein supplementation (including amino acid supplements) for reasons previously mentioned.

Fluid intake is extremely important to the training and racing biathlete. Almost all biochemical processes require or take place in the presence of good old H2O. Dehydration, in addition to being potentially life threatening, is a major cause of diminished performance in long races and training sessions. Consciously consume as much water, or liquids containing water, as you can throughout the course of your day, and then particularly on long training runs and rides. Don't drink so much that you have to relieve yourself every twenty minutes or so - just experiment and find your optimum fluid intake. Better to find out your limitations now than in a race. You may think it wise to go on an occasional long run or ride without water. Wrong. Don't sacrifice recovery from training days thinking that dehydration will make you stronger or prepare you for a race without water. It just doesn't work that way and any sanctioned race worth its salt should have more than adequate fluid on the course.

Fuel consumption during long training rides and races lasting more than two hours can also spell the difference between success and failure. One obvious way to postpone glycogen depletion is to consume more glycogen during the actual event. Keep in mind that there is a significant amount of time between ingestion, absorption and utilization of the fuel you consume on the go. It is important to experiment with what foods work, how long they take to work and how much you can comfortably ingest without causing stomach problems or cramps. Muffins, figs, baked potatoes, bananas and dried fruits are popular and work well. There are also several products specifically intended to be consumed during workouts and races. Some are in fluid form and contain complex carbohydrates and electrolytes in solution. Others, like Powerbars, are solid versions of these nutrients designed to absorb slowly and steadily into the digestive tract with the help of water. I prefer the solid form because it prevents that empty-stomach feeling. You may find otherwise, but whichever you choose, always consume something on a regular basis on rides over two hours. Train your body to handle food intake on the fly and you'll extend that limited glycogen supply.

STRETCHING

I have never been a big fan of stretching. It is time-consuming and not tremendously exciting. However, some stretching is probably beneficial to the warm-up and cooling down process of hard workouts and, according to some physical therapists, aids in recovery time. In fact, many exercise physiologists maintain that, of the three main components of fitness (strength, endurance and flexibility), it is flexibility that becomes the most important as we get older. That argument also includes the notion that the greater the range of motion a biathlete has in his leg muscles, the more ground he can cover.

Over the years, I have found that, for longer aerobic efforts, a gradual warming up on either the bike or the run is sufficient to stretch the muscles before finding your workout pace. Just ease into the workout. I have seen several cases of pre-workout stretching of cold muscles actually result in muscle tightness - the opposite of the desired effect. If you do decide to stretch before a workout, my recommendation is to first do some easy running or riding for 10 minutes, then stop and stretch while the muscles are warm. Then continue with the main body of your workout. I also recommend light stretching when track work is called for just after your easy one- to two-mile warm-up.

The best and probably most beneficial time to stretch is AFTER your workout, while the muscles are warm and supple. A post-workout stretch is probably what leaves you ready to begin the next workout with just an easy warm-up. If you decide to forego that stretching period, be sure at least to do some brief warm-down spinning or

SAMPLE STRETCHES:

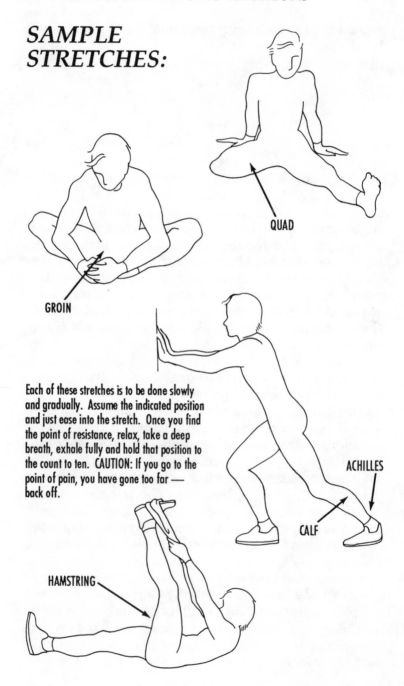

QUAD

GROIN

Each of these stretches is to be done slowly and gradually. Assume the indicated position and just ease into the stretch. Once you find the point of resistance, relax, take a deep breath, exhale fully and hold that position to the count to ten. CAUTION: If you go to the point of pain, you have gone too far — back off.

ACHILLES

CALF

HAMSTRING

jogging before you hit the showers.

REST

I refer to rest frequently in the preceding pages, but have not yet touched upon exactly what constitutes quality rest. Is it sleep? Does it just refer to the time you are not working out? How much is enough?

My definition of quality rest is that which allows you to recover enough to build back stronger before you go out and hammer again. Certainly, adequate sleep is of extreme importance. As we are already all too well aware, every BODY is different. While six hours sleep may be more than enough for some people, nine hours is not enough for others. Our sleep requirements also depend heavily on other factors in our lives like job requirements, family obligations, psychological frame of mind, etc. It is ironic also that sometimes overtraining can cause lack of sleep when, in fact, sleep is most crucial to recovery. In other cases, athletes can sleep too much and training can suffer as a result. Have you ever noticed that sometimes the more sleep you get, the more you want?

By recording the number of hours sleep you get and experimenting with increasing or decreasing amounts, you can determine what works optimally for you. Much to my own surprise, I found several years ago that six and a half hours during light training and seven and a half during my heaviest weeks were all I needed. Any less or any more left me feeling not quite as sharp the next day. Since then I have had many athletes do a two or three month experiment to discover optimum sleep requirements. Many find that they need less than they had assumed. And the discipline of conducting the experiment benefitted their training schedules. You need to record times religiously and trust your alarm clock to get an accurate sense of how much sleep you need.

Some of these same athletes have found also that a one-hour nap, if the schedule allows, assists greatly in recovery when they are unable to get their full amount of night sleep. My only caution about naps is to keep them under 90 minutes. Any more than that and the body begins to make preparations for a full night of sleep.

Quality rest also means that during your non-work-out waking hours you are not putting any additional physical strains on yourself that would interfere with recovery. Recreational activities like playing tennis or basketball (even though these are not specific to biathlon training) will interfere with recovery. Working a hard physical job like moving or construction will do the same. Plan your hard workout days to be followed by easy work or easy recreation days if possible.

Mental stress can also interfere with recovery in a very physical way. In this hectic society, our fight or flight responses to work and social challenges often strain our immune system and our adrenals the same way training and racing do. Take time to consciously relax at work or at home. If you own a heart monitor you can even use biofeedback to lower your heart rate, blood pressure and breathing when you find yourself over-responding to the rigors of the real world.

One of the time-tested indicators of overtraining and the necessity for more recovery time is the monitoring of your resting pulse. If you record resting pulse (RP) daily in your training log you should notice that, as fitness increases, RP decreases for a while and then, at some low point, levels off. RP should be taken just upon waking, while still in bed and lying down. Just look over at your clock or watch, take a quick 15-second wrist or neck count and multiply by four. An RP that is 10 beats higher than your normal RP is a sign of overtraining and the need to take a day off or at least very easy.

VISUALIZATION

Much has been written about visualization over the past few years. Some coaches swear by it, others dismiss it as so much voodoo mumbo jumbo. I find that there are some good aspects to it and it certainly would not hurt some athletes to try one or two exercises. The danger of relying too heavily on visualization is that sometimes one part of the brain is just too smart to believe what another part of the brain is trying to tell it. For example, repeating the positive affirmation: "Every day in every way I am getting better and better," is a common self-improvement exercise. But more often than not, the smart part of the brain, that little devil on your shoulder, might be saying, "Bull, I am NOT and I'll prove it," and the affirmation can work against you.

On the other hand, swim coaches use visualization effectively to aid in neuromuscular patterning of stroke technique because it is something that both halves of the brain can get behind and believe in. In this example, the athlete visualizes a clear picture of a perfect stroke and then executes the stroke in minute detail over and over in the mind before putting it into practice in the pool. You can do the same with track running technique.

Another example can be very helpful for your racing focus. Lie down in a quiet spot for about 15 minutes occasionally and visualize the next race, especially if you know the course well, going over the race in your mind step by step and filing it away as a master plan. This plan can then be referred to during the actual race and, we hope, followed exactly. There is a theory that the mind will not let us do anything that it cannot conceive of us doing and that by making the race real in your mind you are "allowing" yourself to play it out. As far-fetched as this may seem, think about what happens at the cutting edge of human performance. The world record in the marathon stood at 2:08:38 for over 10 years. When it was finally broken by Alberto Salazar, every other top runner realized "intellectually" that it was indeed possible to do. That record has now fallen many times over the past few years. Salazar allowed everyone else to push the envelope. But first he had to visualize himself doing it.

On a daily basis I use visualization to deal with small demons. One person I coach has a real phobia about riding into a headwind and it actually slows her down much more than it should. I have her visualize while she's riding that the wind is a huge blanket, and when she gets low (aero) on her bike, the blanket goes right over her and she passes underneath unaffected.

Many biathletes experience what can only be described as "noise" in their heads when high-level training efforts are called for. The noise is actually a random firing of thoughts in the brain saying, "stop, slow down, this is not good to do, I'm overheating." Remember that at the survival level, it is the job of the brain to tell you to stop, that this activity is consuming valuable energy and poses a threat. We know intellectually, however, that we can handle the load and that there is in fact no threat to survival. But that won't stop the noise. By focusing intensely on the immediate task ahead of us we can sometimes quiet the mind down. Occasionally, however, stronger measures are called for, and this is where visualization can help.

The process I use involves lying in a restful place with the lights out and no outside noise. The first few minutes are spent clearing the mind and just relaxing every muscle in the body. Now begin by identifying all the sensations associated with a particularly "noisy" workout. Let's use a hill-climb interval session as an example. What happens to the legs during the work interval? How about the breathing? Body temperature? Is there any pounding in the head? At what time does the noise start? Now start to experience all these sensations from the comfort of your bed or couch.

After you have identified and experienced the sensations and have a clear picture in your mind, begin to fill the perimeter of that picture in your mind with little chunks of pure clear crystal. Once you have filled the perimeter, start now to fill in the rest of the field of vision you are imagining with more of those crystals until you have systematically filled the entire field. Notice that the noise has disappeared and is now on the other side of your crystal "window". Your breathing is regular, your legs feel powerful, not weak or tired, and you are totally in command of your strength as you climb the hill. Enjoy that experience for a few moments and then slowly come out of your visualization process.

After a few sessions of this exercise, you will have some new associations with what you used to perceive as painful and noisy. Now when things begin to descend on you in a workout or a race, visualize your crystal window and find your focus.

SUMMARY

My intention in this book has been to simplify the often-confusing process of training for biathlon competitions. It is quite possible that any program you stick to will produce some measurable results, but my goal is to provide the shortest, safest and most effective route possible to your peak performance. I have intentionally left out the history, politics, photographs and personality profiles of this sport so that we could get right down to business. If you can retain and "own" the following points we have covered in this book, you will be miles and minutes ahead of your competition:

- Familiarize yourself with the basic training concepts

- Pay attention to individual workouts - not weekly mileage

- Do YOUR workouts - not someone else's

- Monitor and record your heart rate, times and distances

- Spend at least the minimum amount of time in each training phase before moving on to the next phase

- Allow for quality rest - avoid overtraining

- When in doubt, take a day off

- Maintain form and technique in training and in races

- Eat a diet high in complex carbohydrates, low in fats

- Drink plenty of water

- Race fast and have fun

— *Good luck.*

BIBLIOGRAPHY

Astrand, Per-Olaf and Rodahl, Kaare. Textook of Work Physiology, New York: McGraw-Hill, 1977.

Costill, David. Inside Running, Indianapolis: Benchmark Press, 1986.

Costill, David. A Scientific Approach to Distance Running. Los Altos, CA: Track and Field News, 1979.

Hooker, Gary. "Monitoring Your Training," Competitor, February 1988. Del Mar, CA: Competitor, Inc., 1988.

McCardle, William; Katch, Frank and Katch, Victor. Exercise Physiology, Philadelphia: Lea and Febiger, 1986.

Sisson, Mark. Triathlon Training Book, New York: Macmillan, 1983.

Van Handle, Peter. "Fundamentals of the New Training," Bike Tech, Winter 1986. Emmaus, PA: Rodale Press, 1986.

Van Handle, Peter. "Periodization of Training," Bike Tech, April 1987. Emmaus, PA: Rodale Press, 1987.

Van Handle, Peter. "Specificity of Training," Bike Tech, June 1987, Emmaus, PA: Rodale Press, 1987.

FRACTIONAL PACE CHART

10K	5K	10 mi.	MAXIMAL VO2 MAX TEST			THRESHOLD 95%		90%		85%		80%		BASE 75%		70%		SUB-MAX TEST	
			H.R.	PACE	1/4 mi.	H.R.	PACE	H.R.	PACE	H.R.	PACE	H.R.	PACE	H.R.	PACE	H.R.	PACE	PACE	%
30:00	14:20	50:10		4:30	67		4:35		5:00		5:20		5:45		6:10		6:35	5:30	
30:30	14:30	50:45		4:30	68		4:35		5:00		5:20		5:45		6:10		6:35	5:30	
31:00	14:45	51:45		4:35	69		4:45		5:10		5:30		5:55		6:20		6:45	5:30	
31:30	15:00	52:25		4:40	70		4:50		5:15		5:35		6:00		6:25		6:50	6:00	
32:00	15:15	53:20		4:45	71		4:55		5:20		5:45		6:10		6:35		7:00	6:00	
32:30	15:30	54:10		4:50	72		5:00		5:25		5:50		6:15		6:40		7:05	6:00	
33:00	15:45	54:55		4:55	73		5:05		5:30		5:55		6:20		6:45		7:10	6:00	
33:30	15:55	55:41		5:00	75		5:10		5:35		6:00		6:25		6:50		7:15	6:00	
34:00	16:10	56:40		5:00	75		5:15		5:40		6:05		6:30		6:55		7:20	6:30	
34:30	16:25	57:25		5:05	77		5:20		5:45		6:10		6:35		7:00		7:25	6:30	
35:00	16:40	58:30		5:10	78		5:20		5:50		6:15		6:40		7:05		7:30	6:30	
35:30	16:50	59:10		5:15	79		5:25		5:55		6:20		6:45		7:10		7:35	6:30	
36:00	17:05	1:00:00		5:20	80		5:30		6:00		6:25		6:50		7:15		7:40	6:30	
36:30	17:15	1:00:50		5:25	81		5:35		6:05		6:30		6:55		7:20		7:45	6:30	
37:00	17:35	1:01:40		5:30	82		5:40		6:10		6:35		7:00		7:25		7:50	6:30	
37:30	17:50	1:02:35		5:35	84		5:45		6:15		6:45		7:10		7:35		8:00	7:00	
38:00	18:05	1:03:35		5:35	85		5:50		6:20		6:50		7:15		7:40		8:05	7:00	
38:30	18:15	1:04:10		5:40	86		5:55		6:25		6:55		7:20		7:45		8:10	7:00	
39:00	18:30	1:05:00		5:45	87		6:00		6:30		7:00		7:25		7:50		8:15	7:00	
39:30	18:45	1:05:40		5:50	88		6:00		6:35		7:05		7:30		7:55		8:20	7:00	
40:00	19:00	1:06:45		5:55	89		6:05		6:40		7:10		7:35		8:00		8:25	7:00	
41:00	19:30	1:08:25		6:05	91		6:15		6:50		7:20		7:45		8:10		8:35	7:30	
42:00	20:00	1:10:10		6:15	93		6:25		7:00		7:30		7:55		8:20		8:45	7:30	
43:00	20:25	1:11:50		6:25	95		6:35		7:10		7:40		8:05		8:30		8:55	7:30	
44:00	20:55	1:13:30		6:35	98		6:40		7:20		7:50		8:15		8:40		9:05	7:30	
45:00	21:20	1:15:15		6:45	101		6:50		7:30		8:00		8:25		8:50		9:15	8:00	
46:00	21:45	1:17:00		6:55	104		7:00		7:40		8:10		8:35		9:05		9:25	8:00	
47:00	22:10	1:18:45		7:05	106		7:10		7:50		8:20		8:45		9:15		9:35	8:00	
48:00	22:40	1:20:15		7:15	109		7:20		8:00		8:30		8:50		9:25		9:45	8:00	
49:00	23:10	1:22:00		7:25	111		7:25		8:10		8:40		9:05		9:35		9:55	8:00	
50:00	23:40	1:23:45		7:35	113		7:35		8:20		8:50		9:20		9:45		10:00	8:00	

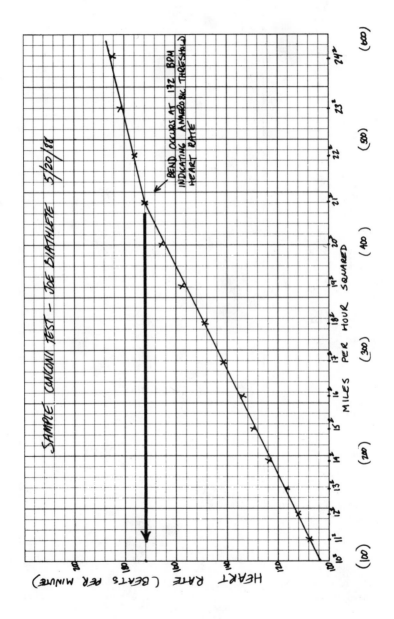

Date _APRIL 26_   Training Phase _STRENGTH_   Week # _3_

Max HR _190_   Recent Submaximal Efficiency _77%_   Weight _152_

Resting Pulse _48_   (BT)   BE   AR   Day off

Workout Goal: _EASY WARM-UP ON BIKE, 5 RIDING HILL REPEATS_
UP PALISADES HIGHLANDS.

Working Heart Rate Goal _170_

Workout Results: _5 REPEATS IN 9:55, 10:03, 9:38, 10:14, 10:12_

Actual Workout Heart Rate _172_

Comments: _SLIGHT HEADWIND, FELT GREAT ON FIRST THREE, REALLY_
BEAT ON LAST TWO. RECOVERED EASILY ON 10-MILE WARM DOWN.

Date _____ Training Phase _____ Week # ___

Max HR _____ Recent Submaximal Efficiency _____ Weight ___

Resting Pulse _____   BT   BE   AR   Day off

Workout Goal:

Working Heart Rate Goal _____

Workout Results:

Actual Workout Heart Rate _____

Comments:

NOTES